HOMOSEXUALITY
HETEROSEXUALITY
PERVERSION

HOMOSEXUALITY
HETEROSEXUALITY
PERVERSION

Fritz Morgenthaler

with an Introduction by
Werner Muensterberger, Ph.D.

translated from the German by
Andreas Aebi, Ph.D.

edited by
Paul Moor

THE ANALYTIC PRESS

1988   Hillsdale, NJ   Hove and London

Originally published as *Homosexualität Heterosexualität Perversion*
© 1984 Qumran Verlag

The Analytic Press.
Distributed solely by

Lawrence Erlbaum Associates, Inc., Publishers
365 Broadway
Hillsdale, New Jersey 07642

Library of Congress Cataloging-in-Publication Data

Morgenthaler, Fritz, 1919–1984
  Homosexuality, heterosexuality, perversion.

  Translation of: Homosexualität, Heterosexualität,
Perversion.
  Includes bibliographies and index.
  1. Homosexuality—Psychological aspects.
2. Sexual deviation—Treatment.   3. Psychoanalysis.
I. Moor, Paul, 1924-   . II. Title. [DNLM:
1. Homosexuality.   2. Paraphilias.   3. Psychoanalysis.
WM 610 M851h]
RC558.M6513   1987   616.85'834   87-18698
ISBN 0-88163-060-8

Printed in the United States of America

10   9   8   7   6   5   4   3   2   1

CONTENTS

INTRODUCTION

by Werner Muensterberger

The central theme of *Homosexuality, Heterosexuality, Perversion* is controversial and historically has given rise to partisan sympathies and prejudices. The book concerns the varieties of sexual experiences and how we go about determining which is "normal" and which "pathological," or rather which is "conflict free" and which is rooted in conflict. Fritz Morgenthaler (1919–1984) pursued issues of psychosexual experience with inquiring rigor and objectivity.

The volume is the outgrowth of a series of lectures and articles that Morgenthaler delivered and published between 1960 and 1983. He subsequently reworked them for the present publication. After decades of painstaking clinical observations and extensive ethnopsychoanalytic field research, he and his colleagues, Paul Parin and Goldy Parin-Matthèy, together arrived at pathmaking conclusions that were essential for Morgenthaler's further clinical work. Both the clinical work itself and the challenging theoretical considerations to which it gave rise are elaborated in *Homosexuality, Heterosexuality, Perversion*.

Trained as a physician specializing in neurology and psychiatry, Morgenthaler soon came to psychoanalysis. For him, however, psychoanalysis was not simply a method of mental treatment. He was a highly sensitive man who, by the way, was also an accomplished and widely recognized painter. His keen social conscience made him acutely aware of the influence of cultural values, vices, and virtues on individual development and individual sensibilities.

He understood the essential link between traditional ideologies and milieu-bound constraints, and also the relevance of such values and the vicissitudes of culture-bound constraints on critical emotional constellations, i.e., their significance for the individual psychic structures of ego and superego.

Not being blinded by Western man's blinkers and hence recognizing a correlation between Judeo-Christian mores, clinical assessment, and alternative conceptualizations, Morgenthaler sought different sources of information. His careful monitoring of the impact of culturally defined traditional aims and his emphases on treatment goals made him aware of the effect of these same aims and concerns on diagnostic findings and alternative explanations. In brief, Morgenthaler came to appreciate the vital role of the sociocultural and historical background in the interpretation and evaluation of clinical data. As ethnopsychoanalysts we tend to have a more vivid picture of the array of complementary currents between the growing child and the principal agents of a particular environment than does the clinician working in a comparative narrowly demarcated and segmented milieu. Much clinical research and an impressive amount of otherwise well-documented descriptive data show little awareness of culture-specific adaptive variables and the observer's own conceptual leanings. But once, like Morgenthaler, we venture outside these protecting confines, we gain a broader perspective that belies what psychoanalysts are accustomed to call (after Heinz Hartmann's misunderstood and not very lucky formulation) "the average expectable environment."

These distinctions furnish the elements for Morgenthaler's ethnopsychoanalytic outlook, and especially for his reassessment of psychoanalytic propositions with respect to perversions, homosexuality, and variations of sexual excitation. After many years of clinical work in Switzerland, he became sensitized to significant differences in interpersonal relationships among his patients; the variable roles of shame and guilt in such relationships, especially among people whose basic defenses—e.g., projection, disavowal, denial, isolation—are significantly involved in behavior patterns, beliefs and culture-specific creative and regulative functions, are but one example.

To what alternatives does the analyst have recourse? Can our inquiries be objective as long as they, not surprisingly, collude with certain culture-bound reference systems and sentiments? In search of more evidence of the effect of developmental forces within different sociocultural traditions, he set out with the Parins to conduct ethnopsychoanalytic field research in West Africa, first among the Dogon in Mali and later among the Anyi in the Ivory Coast. Their case studies, carried out in the field, led to strikingly illuminating comparisons. Via a carefully adapted psychoanalytic research method, they arrived at new formulations about significant variations in ego development and ego differentiation, variations that bear on fundamental aspects of individual lives, on psychic structure, and that gain expression in certain facets of object relatedness.

It should be understood that divergent cultural environments give rise to different preoedipal conditions, identifications, ideals, and concepts of self. Consider, for example, the astonishing variety of types of mothering quite unexpected in Western society (see Muensterberger, 1974). We know of societies where breast-feeding is not terminated before the fourth or even fifth year, and skin contact between mother and child is continued far longer than in the Western world, where, as Spitz (1957, pp. 124 f.) has stressed, this kind of intimacy has been artificially reduced, "probably with damaging results." Consequently, postponement of weaning and separation of the infant from the mother will have an effect on the child's psychic and emotional development (cf. Spitz, 1957, p. 124, n. 2). It follows that the dynamic factors that account for the makeup of the self often lead to a different implementation of the defenses that Western man takes more or less for granted. Different experiential conditions account for patterns in the social sphere that emphasize dependency relationships frequently worlds apart from our individualistic norms and expectations. (Jacques Lacan felt that it was the invention of the mirror that facilitated Western man's ever-increasing self-absorption.) This tallies with an early observation of Freud's that acknowledges such vital sociocultural differences. In a footnote of 1910 to "Three Essays on The Theory of Sexuality" (1905), Freud observed that "the most striking distinction between the erotic life of antiquity and our own no doubt lies in the fact that the ancients laid stress upon the instinct itself, whereas we emphasize its object. The ancients glorified the instinct, while we despise the instinctual activity itself, and find excuses for it only in the merits of the object," (p. 149). Thus, Freud understood heterosexuality in ancient cultures as straightforward genital excitation and endpleasure free from any affection or the luxury of tenderness and indulgence in foreplay, the latter being refinements of the *artes amandi* of which the Romans were aware.

It must be stressed that by decoding the variations of lovemaking, psychoanalysis has shown that all kinds of forepleasure are composed of elements that, were they not associated with orgasmic endpleasure, might well be diagnosed as a perversion. This insight, in turn, brings us to the crucial question, posed by Freud, of how far "sexual repression as an internal factor alongside such external factors as limitation of freedom, inaccessability of a normal sex object, the dangers of the normal sexual act, etc., bring about perversions..." (Freud, 1905, p. 170). Here Freud grants that both internal and environmental factors effect innumerable facets of psychosexual experience. He cites the example of ancient Greece as one culture-specific instance "where the most masculine men were numbered among the inverts" (p. 144). In more recent years, a research team of American psychoanalysts arrived at a quite similar conclusion: "Under certain cultural conditions and when it exists without the qualities of compulsion and fixity, homosexual behavior need not necessarily be perverse" (Ostow et al., 1974, p. 4). While a number of psychoanalysts have agreed in principle with Freud's position that "psychoanalytic research is most decidedly opposed to any attempt at separating off homosexuals from the rest of mankind as a group of a special character" (Freud, 1905, p. 145), the issue remains controversial. Many analysts, even Freud in certain instances, failed to recognize the distinction between norm and normality (Muensterberger, 1956) by taking their own culture as a model.

Such were the issues the Parins and Morgenthaler attempted to study in various different societies. In further pursuit of his comparative ethnopsychoanalytic research, Morgenthaler proceeded to South America and Madagascar. With his son Marco, an anthropologist, he conducted additional fieldwork among the Iatmul in the Sepik area of New Guinea. The Iatmul have been well known since Gregory Bateson's (1936) pioneering research of their institutionalized and tribally demanded transvestitism.

The novel propositions with which Morgenthaler emerged from his field observations are anything but armchair conclusions. It is his contention that many aspects of the analysand's predicament reflect the interplay between intrapsychic affectivity and maladaptation within a given environment. Moreover, he saw the influence of traditional, i.e., Judeo-Christian, ethics and values even in theoretical psychoanalytic precepts, propositions, and interpretive explanations.

For Morgenthaler, and for psychoanalytic anthropology in general, measuring a native's libidinal strivings, interpersonal relationships, and defensive structures, let alone autonomous ego functions, according to Western scales is to take a position reminiscent of that of the early missionaries, who came to the eternal rescue of aborigines because anything but the belief in Christian doctrines was considered heathen. Indeed, for a Westerner unacquainted with the psychic dispositions and emotional lives of natives, it is not easy to gauge their private experience, especially their values and conflicts. Observing these people in their own habitat, we see how different patterns of interaction, first between mother and infant and subsequently between the baby and the larger environment, account for psychic modalities often surprisingly dissimiliar from anything we would ordinarily expect. For example, we now know of many tribes in Africa, in the South Seas, and the Americas where certain transvestite practices are institutionalized. Morgenthaler applies his newly won insights about such practices in discussing his treatment of a brilliant writer whose developmental conflicts led him to transvestitism and passive homosexual encounters. The analyst, after having conducted field research among the Iatmul, revised his point of view vis-à-vis this man's state of mind. Recognizing his own ethnocentric prejudice, he was led to reinterpret the particular variables that entered into his patient's leanings. In the case of the people of New Guinea, ritualized transvestitism served as a sensory mode of reinforcing body ego and body identity. And Morgenthaler discovered that his Swiss patient's obsessional dressing in female garments fulfilled the same function. It was the man's way to adapt, in a primary-process fashion, his illusionary creative achievement to the conditions of his environment. What the Iatmul dramatize in their transvestite ceremonies this patient attempted to act out in his, to us, perverse impersonation.

Morgenthaler reminds his readers that the clinical data on which psychoanalysis bases its arguments, especially with regard to sexual practices that are not in accordance with Western moral standards, have implicit disadvantages, for they rely on information from the limited group of conflict-ridden patients. These facts are bound not only to obliterate the psychosociocultural reality, but to blur a constructive distinction between neurotic and unconflicted homosexuality. Needless to say, this is hardly the most advantageous starting point for understanding a phenomenon that is fully integrated and conflict free within the moral concerns of different sociocultural systems.

The present work, then, takes a novel route. Morgenthaler's research and explorations focus on alternative interpretations of aspects of psychosexual phenomena. He approaches human sexuality from a nonconflictual angle, simply presupposing a natural condition of inner harmony. In terms of his hypothesis, ego development and libido organization are powerfully influenced by the prevailing cultural ethos. It is this unequivocal position that leads him to new, persuasive psychoanalytic insights and alternative criteria for distinguishing between the "normal" and the "perverse."

References

Bateson, G. (1936): *Naven,* Cambridge University Press, Cambridge, MA.

Freud, S. (1905): Three essays on the theory of sexuality, in: *Standard Edition* 7 (135–243).

Muensterberger, W. (1956): Perversion, cultural norm and normality, in: S. Lorand & M. Balint (ed.) *Perversions: Psychodynamics and Therapy,* Random House, New York, pp. 55–67.

———— (1974): Some reflections on multiple mothering, cross-culturally, in: *Psychosocial Process* 3(57–71).

Ostow, M. et al. (1974): *Sexual Deviation: Psychoanalytic Insights.* Quadrangle, New York.

Spitz, R. A. (1957): *No and Yes,* International Universities Press, New York.

1

THE PRACTICE OF PSYCHOANALYSIS

When studying psychoanalysis, one can acquire metapsychology, theory of technique, and a collection of proven rules by learning them. Nevertheless, as soon as one attempts to apply psychoanalysis practically with a patient, it retains certain aspects that are difficult to comprehend.

Psychoanalysis cannot be learned by amassing factual knowledge or by cataloguing information one acquires in school. Educational processes in which, on the one hand, an increase in performance is expected and, on the other hand, a premium for success is promised, are anal learning processes, which are contradictory to the essence of psychoanalysis. It is not possible to acquire a usable psychoanalytic technique in this manner.

One essential aspect of psychoanalytic technique consists in the ability to carry out deductions from interpretive steps, anew and independently, during each analytic session. The analyst must be able to make a usable number of choices from a large number of possible interpretations and ideas. Depending on the analyst's mood of the moment, and according to his skills and experiences, these choices will vary. Nevertheless, the selection will always have to be carried out in such a manner that what the analyst says befits his or her personality, and that it helps to establish the relationship with the patient correctly. If one compares the almost inexhaustible choice of possible technical advice with a large catalog from which the selection is made by means of association, it seems impossible to provide any guidelines according to which such a selection is to be made. One will at best realize that this catalog contains much that is beneficial and much that is detrimental to the patient. However, I should like to emphasize particularly that this catalog also contains many beneficial and detrimental aspects for the analyst, who first will have to learn to differentiate between the one and the other.

Young analysts who have completed their own training analyses, and who are having their first experiences with their patients, tend, in general, to reactivate the residue of their own neuroses in their relationships with their analysands. Old conflict tendencies, worked at in their own analyses and seemingly overcome, will reappear. Certain modes of behavior of the analysand can, non-specifically and unobtrusively, trigger tensions in the analyst in which unpleasure dominates. Analysts may find themselves in conflict if the patient is constantly talking or keeping silent, or is expressing open or veiled criticism or praise. Sometimes it is the listening process, at other times the interpretation process that will result in difficulties. In such cases, analysts usually have not been able to adapt themselves to the psychoanalytic situation. The residue of their own neuroses is still "fresh."

In the analytic situation, the conflict tendencies of the analyst decrease with experience. The neurotic residue will become more settled and eventually part of the psychoanalytic personality. But it also becomes part of the individual psychoanalytic technique. By then, the old conflict tendencies are hardly perceived with unpleasure any longer. They reflect a much deeper stratum of the analyst's personality. What is reflected here is the individually very disparate fate of infantile sexual explorations. Expressed in their newfound sublimated form, these explorations belong to the healthy parts of the ego and are in harmony with the mature and nonneurotic personality of the analyst. We have to assume that our own infantile sexual curiosity has become sublimated in the course of our own analysis to the extent that it functions with neutralized energy. Only when this goal has been achieved can psychoanalysis become the new object of curiosity. This new object choice is an unconscious process and consequently has different results with different individuals.

There are analysts who particularly concentrate their interest on investigating the inner life of the analysand. They would most like to content themselves with having understood what is going on in the patient, and they find it tedious to communicate their insights to the analysand. The sublimated infantile sexual exploration still has traits of the pleasure of peeping in early childhood.

The difficulties that may result from this are, in tendency, connected to the fact that these analysts cannot comprehend why they are being loved.

Other analysts are particularly eager to provide the analysand with newly gained insights and to provide interpretations of everything they have perceived of the inner life of their patients. Their comprehension of the structural, dynamic, and economic connections of the development of their patient's conflict is often less differentiated than the perception of their previously mentioned colleagues, but their relationship with their analysands is frequently livelier and more spontaneous. The sublimated sexual curiosity of these analysts still seems to be characterized by an infantile impulsiveness, making it more difficult to overcome a tendency toward motor activity. Analysts of this group often have difficulty in completely comprehending the aggression problems of their analysands, because it is not easy for them to recognize with sufficient clarity the feelings of hatred their patients direct at them.

Another group of analysts can perhaps be characterized as being particularly interested in the consequences of their own behavior and that of their patients, and, furthermore, in making the consequences of the provided interpretation the focus of their attention. These analysts seem relaxed, detached, and neutral. They probably correspond most typically to the image of the classic, didactic training analyst. With these analysts, the instinctual impulses stimulated by the sexual curiosity of childhood, together with the defense mechanisms that had been raised with regard to sexual exploration, have become transformed into a certain form of adaptation, of which the psychoanalytic activity is a sublimated expression. The functional change of the defense is more distinct in their attitude than the sublimation of their instinctual impulses. This, in part, may also be the reason for the fact that these analysts tend to underestimate the effect that their personality radiates.

One could juxtapose this group of analysts with those who seem particularly interested in feeling superior in regard to all expressions and modes of behavior of their analysands. In their childhood, such analysts perhaps became acquainted only with aim-inhibited opportunities when pleasurably conducting their infantile sexual exploration. They probably denied their tendency in that direction from the very beginning. As analysts, they therefore run the risk of overlooking what is really going on in their patient at a specific point during analysis. Under the stress of countertransference, they tend to take the attitude that they already know everything that can move the patient. It often may be difficult for such analysts to recognize how they themselves react to external influences. Likewise, they have difficulty in assessing how their environment reacts to them.

This categorization could easily be continued. However, it was important to me only to emphasize the various differences in analysts in order to demonstrate how each one of us develops individually specific signals in the course of our psychoanalytic activities. These signals trigger—usually preconsciously and by way of association—specific modes of behavior, auxiliary technical models and measures, so that the influence of the analyst's personal peculiarities does not figure too importantly. Whatever these peculiarities might be, many signals in the course of the analytic activity eventually result in the fact that each analyst acquires individual psychoanalytic technique that is based on a collection of proven fundamental rules of technique.

With increased experience, and by getting older, the analyst seems to become ever more secure in his or her analyses. Yet, one particular form of ease that might come with age must not be confused with the acquisition of a logically consistent psychoanalytic technique. That ease was characterized by Reik: "How fortunate that not only the hunted but also the hunters become tired." Indeed, with older analysts the diminished intensity of the drives might contribute to a more tolerant, more secure manner during analyses. In such a case, however, one cannot overlook the fact that the training analysis that the therapist himself or herself underwent at one time did not fulfill its requirements.

If an analyst was insufficiently analyzed during the training period, the effects on his or her technique can be severe. It can happen that in the course of their subsequent activities, insufficiently analyzed analysts borrow a series of auxiliary technical aids from other fields of science, or that they themselves invent them in order to maintain their neurotic equilibrium within the analyses they are conducting. Such technical crutches often have the appearance of actual reaction-formations and represent an instrument for unconscious coacting out. Sometimes such auxiliary aids are structured like true symptoms. Since these measures are unconscious as a rule, and motivated by rationalization, insufficiently analyzed therapists are rarely in a position to judge their new creations in theory and technique objectively.

The process of acquiring an individually suited psychoanalytic technique seems so difficult because the technical procedure must not only take the individual peculiarities of the analyst into account, but must also remain within the framework of a scientifically determinable, generally valid, and controllable psychoanalytic technique.

In a sense, psychoanalytic technique is simultaneously flexible yet rigid; in other words, it is relatively flexible within a determined system. Older analysts with a large amount of experience with training and control analyses quite frequently make this observation: When they are asked, as members of an international committee, to evaluate candidates completely unknown to them, it happens in a remarkably large number of cases that practically all committee members, independently of one another, agree to a great extent in their subjective opinions regarding the capabilities of the candidates, even though the participating analysts may have very disparate opinions among themselves, particularly with regard to the practice of psychoanalytic technique.

The future analyst is often confronted with the difficult question of how, with such premises, one can acquire an adequate technique. How is one to choose, from this almost inexhaustible catalog of offerings, an appropriate selection of those rules of technique which are correct, which one can use, which are suitable for the patient, which take into account the specific situation, and which at the same time make sure that the overly one-sided peculiarities of oneself are balanced in a sensible manner? I believe this complicated question can be reduced to one simple denominator. In every session, day after day, the analyst is confronted by one of the most pressing tasks — to find the proper tone for initiating the communication with the patient. To find the right tone means that the analyst must free the existing, concrete relationship within the analytic hour right then and there from conflict. The most important aid the analyst has available for this task is the analytic situation. It makes it easier for the analyst to direct his or her entire attention to the verbal possibilities from the first analytic hour on, which in turn allows the analyst to attain a non-neurotic attitude even towards a neurotic patient.

If this succeeds, a preconscious selection of the technical aids takes place and usually proves to be right. One cannot expect the "deconflictualization" to be quick and painless. It progresses in small steps and must be established differently with each patient. Often one must wait for days or weeks before one finds access to the patient. If the establishment of a deconflictualized relationship with the analysand is successful, the analyst will have the fascinating experience of having the transference develop transparently and consistently. The conflict tendencies of the patient are then reflected in the analytic relationship in the same patterns in which they had been delineated in his or her childhood.

In the search for the correct approach to the patient, I believe it is especially important to neither equate nor confuse that approach with the actual work of interpretation. As long as we have not succeeded in establishing an *ad hoc* deconflictualized relationship with our analysand, we are unable to provide a reconstructive interpretation. Generally speaking, no interpretation should be given if we have no concept. We should be able to formulate this concept for ourselves first, before we attempt to explain to a patient something about his or her life's history. If we do not respect this rule, we run the risk of acting out in countertransference. Only after we have become better acquainted with the patient can our interpretational concept also be preconscious, or even unconscious. Before we make an interpretation, we should check our own associations regarding the patient's material against our concept. This raises the question of how one can arrive at a concept and how it is formed.

I believe one finds a concept by comparing those processes which become apparent in transference with the material presented by the patient. Based on this comparison, we can guess the conflict tendencies in the childhood of this patient. This concerns only those conflict tendencies of childhood which are reflected exclusively in the transference of this particular time-segment of the analytic process and which become apparent in the relationship with the analyst. In this connection let me emphasize an especially significant experience: If the analysand reports childhood memories that do not seem to fit the concept of the analyst, the concept should not immediately be changed. Often our analysand's memories are screen memories, often also memories from childhood augmented by phantasies. In this regard, another consideration seems even more important to me, namely, that certain memories, told to us during the analytic session by our patient, presage much later segments in the course of the analysis and do not belong to the analytic process of the moment. We have to accept that some correlations communicated by the patient will be understood only much later.

It is my opinion that the analyst's concept must be derived fundamentally from what becomes visible in the transference. Out of the associations and dreams the patient presents for interpretation, the analyst selects only that which is suitable to the transference development. Of course, this succeeds in a meaningful manner only if a continuous deconflictualization during the analytic hour and the affective relaxation of the analytic milieu can be maintained by the analyst. An unneurotic relationship between analyst and patient that is relatively free of conflict is the essential premise for the so-called working alliance. It is possible to fail here, but the analyst remains conscious of what he or she is striving for and where a failure may eventually occur. The establishment of the working alliance is primarily the task of the analyst. From the technical standpoint, it does not provide any particular problem. The difficulties that appear in the pursuit of this task coincide to a large extent with the difficulties the analyst has with the patient. The thesis of a working alliance belongs to that large catalog of technical possibilities from which each individual selects what suits him or her. It might well be that some analysts will make this thesis the focal point of their technical aids. The question here, I feel, depends mainly upon whether, during our own analyses, we have found or created sufficient possibilities in our own personalities to allow us to deal with diverse people without conflict.

Although the requirements for a meaningful application of psychoanalytic technique may seem indefinable yet circumscribed, their fundamental characteristics are clear and simple. The means of which psychoanalysts make use are means they need in order to be able to react to their patients in an unneurotic manner. These means differ from individual to individual and depend upon our own residual neurosis, even though it no longer disturbs us. The distant aim of freeing our analysand from his neurotic development actually does not concern us much. The immediate aim, which we strive for day after day in every analytic hour, is the affective *relaxation* of the relationship between the analyst and the analysand. Then—in my opinion—the transference neurosis will emerge clear and recognizable in its conformity to the rules. If the influence of the patient's unconscious superego demands, as well as the influence of the analyst, on the analysis itself, could be estimated to be less than it actually is, one obviously would have fewer difficulties in circumscribing more precisely what is important in the application of psychoanalysis as a method of therapy. The conscious and unconscious demands of the superego, however, are much more significant during the analytic treatment than one often thinks. The patients who come to us for treatment would like to be good analysands. They would like to do everything right, and they suffer when they discover flaws in their behavior that remind them that they cannot always do what they would like to do. Within their striving to complete their analysis, analysands are actually being guided by strong, unconscious demands of conscience.

In general, analysts tend to appreciate particularly their patients' positive attitude towards the analysis and the patient's willingness to cooperate. They justifiably place value on this attitude in their patients, for it is one of the most important premises for analysis in general. Analysts themselves have, almost inevitably, ideals and demands of conscience similar to those of the analysand. They, too, would like to do it right. They, too, find it painful when they do not succeed in conducting the analysis as they wished. They would like to be good analysts who are successful and who remain aware of their responsibility.

The conscious and unconscious superego demands overshadow the course of the analytic process. If the analysis progresses painfully and slowly or in unstructured fashion over long periods, demands of conscience and guilt feelings weigh heavily on the course of the analysis. If the analysis proceeds smoothly and successfully, the analyst quickly, and unwittingly, becomes the authority. The analysand idealizes the "doctor." If analysts react nonneurotically to the analysand, and if their interpretations are correct, they become solid authority figures, and the idealization that the analysand develops towards the analyst detaches itself from the compulsion to repeat early infantile wishes. The idealization now has become a reality. The analyst notes that interpretation does not help in this development, for if the interpretation is correct, it results in further admiration and idealization in the patient, which will survive even a critical examination of reality. It is not unusual for this process to be gradually reversed only long after a thoroughly successful, completed analysis. In my experience with many patients, the creative forces of the secondary autonomous ego functions developed during analysis do not become manifest until long after completion of the analysis. Although all the necessary conditions existed, the productive, creative forces were hindered in finding expression during the analysis due to the superego role of the analyst.

During the course of analyses we conduct with our patients, disturbances in associative freedom, inhibitions of fantasy, and disturbances in expression of various types are frequently determined by the fact that an unspoken, barely recognizable competition between analyst and patient is taking place, which strives to maintain unconscious superego demands with regard to the analysis itself. In order to counter this danger, hardly governable by means of technique, analysts will constantly have to be aware that they should analyze by means of the ego functions, not by means of the superego.

2

THE POSITION OF PERVERSIONS IN METAPSYCHOLOGY AND TECHNIQUE

A relatively short time ago I experienced the ruin of a brilliant, barely 35-year-old writer who had the most extreme form of a manifest sadomasochistic perversion I have ever seen. Subsequent to a very carefully planned encounter with his sadistic partner, who provided him with the physical and psychological degradation he desired and with whom he was able to appease his homosexual desire, he fell into an altered state of mind, and burned down two houses after completely destroying all the household goods he had found in them. After this deed, he lay in wait for people who might appear in the remoteness of the alpine valley where his objects were burning in the mist of fog banks. While waiting he fantasized strangling and stabbing scenes until suddenly, cool and detached, he drove his car home, in no way attracting the attention of those about him. He felt psychologically healthy and was able to do professionally whatever he intended, to feel genuine warmth in his relationships, and to be loving with his wife and son. He was arrested, confined, evaluated, and sentenced. Unbroken, and convinced that he could be cured by means of psychoanalysis, he developed an intensive activity at the psychiatric clinic; he wrote articles and essays that were regularly published. He radiated a peculiar fascination, which drew the staff and the doctors into a barely perceptible, euphoric willingness to accommodate the patient in every way possible. In the clinic he participated in group therapy, soon seduced a woman patient, was taken into individual therapy, and finally was sent for psychoanalytic treat-

10

ment outside the clinic. However, the female analyst somewhat rashly terminated the analytic treatment after eight sessions. Something eerie hung over this case. I was called as a consultant and realized that an ambulatory psychoanalytic treatment was contraindicated. The patient understood and was willing to stay voluntarily at the clinic and obey all directives. A female physician and, soon thereafter, a male colleague agreed to work with the patient under my supervision. The therapists did not feel up to the task. They were afraid, and their fears were justified. The patient was confident, impulsive, direct, affectively involved, and able to attain insight. He put little flowers into his curly hair when he came to a session. Then, one Sunday morning, completely unexpectedly, he took his own life.

Our art does not suffice to help all patients willing to undergo psychonalysis. As a rule, we decide whether treatment is indicated and agree to get involved in a psychoanalysis only if and when we can assume that the analytic process will get under way meaningfully. But I ask: What does it mean, getting an analytic process meaningfully under way when psychosexual disturbances are apparent that during the course of development have become condensed into manifestly perverse syndromes?

I would like to begin by answering this question indirectly: There exists no immediate relationship between a progressive deepening of the analytic process and a possible loosening, flexibility, and reversibility of the perversion that one may have come to expect. This, then, implies the conclusion, which seems important to me, that eliminating the perversion cannot be the aim of the psychoanalytic treatment. Analysis is not a declaration of war against perversion, but a process leading to the most extensive understanding possible of the function that the manifestly perverse activity assumes within the framework of the interactions of the psychic systems with the self.

Important though it is to examine perverse patients in accordance with the pathogenic point of view—that is, examine the developmental disturbances and the defects in the ego and in the narcissistic area in order to explain the fates that the instincts are experiencing—what one captures in this way is, in essence, only the character neuroses, the narcissistic defects, depressions, somatic disturbances, and so forth, that these patients in many cases manifest as concomitant symptoms in addition to their perversion. In order to understand the function of a perversion, another aspect has to be brought into the foreground: A symptom that is pathological when viewed in a transverse section, where it can be traced back to deficiency symptoms in specific developmental phases, is, from a longitudinal view, which includes the total development of the personality, the best possible solution for an optimal interaction of the psychic systems with the self (Hartmann, 1954). Admittedly, the best possible solution for an optimal interaction of the psychic systems can be lethal.

The fate of the writer who succumbed to the malignancy of his perversion cannot discourage me from maintaining the concept that a perversion can be regarded as an ego attainment of a special kind, which, established in early childhood, becomes manifest as a completely formed perversion during adolescence or in adulthood. The writer's fate was cited only as a warning that we must pursue this concept without illusions and that we must not promise ourselves or our patients a more favorable outcome of our psychoanalytic efforts than hitherto expected. The example of the perverse writer, however, provides the opportunity to emphasize a further point of view. I am referring to the quantitative aspect. The vehemence with which the impulse of the sexual instinct asserts itself and amalgamates with the most diverse sexual objects, the sudden transition from a state of sexual excitation to a state of relative instinctual calm, and the ability of these patients to observe and describe the sick, perverse part of their personality by means of the psychically healthy part, present quantitative reinforcements of phenomena characteristic of all people.

If I have just emphasized that a symptom—no matter how pathological it might be when viewed as a transverse section—is a creative attainment of the ego, creating the optimal conditions for the maintenance of a relative psychic equilibrium, I certainly have not characterized the specificity of the perversion. Every symptom can be understood as a creative attainment of the ego. I suggest that here, too, the quantitative moment plays a decisive role. This point of view is of particular importance with regard to perversions.

One may say that every analysis we conduct has its own, individually specific legitimacy. In the analyses with perverted patients, however, this self-contained legitimacy is so pronounced that the course of these analyses in no way follows the conceptions the analyst has derived from the relevant and theoretically established pathogenesis.

All analyses show that a deviation in behavior is not identical with what is experienced in the unconscious. In the case of perverted patients, however, it is of foremost interest to demonstrate that the form of deviation from the normal sexual life cannot be the fundamental issue. In fact, it becomes evident that the instinctual gratification, which perverted patients seek in peculiar rituals and arrangements, while indeed representing a regressive formation of a striving for pleasure and gratification, is in itself subject to a change of function.

Here again it may be said that every instinctual gratification is subject to a functional change to the extent that it normally serves the maintenance of the narcissistic homeostasis. However, what perverse patients strive for in reaching their sexual aims, which they cathect with extraordinary stubbornness, is by no means instinctual gratification but rather the maintenance of their desexualized object relationships: their aim-inhibited, tender feelings, their ideal-formation and ambitions within the social framework in which they live and to which they have adapted. The perverse patients' sense of self-value, their sense of identity, also with regard to their sexual role, depends quite decisively on the maintenance of all those ego functions and libidinal cathexes which were formed—as though detached from the sexual syndrome of their perversion—in the overall development of their personality. For the analyst it is important to know that what the patient portrays as instinctual gratification has another significance. The functional change, on which the instinctual act of the perverse patient is based, is so predominant that the instinctual gratification itself is not only secondary but also, in most cases, notably little cathected, undervalued, or even negligible.

I have thus described a series of generally valid conformities of the human psyche that would not really be characteristic as phenomena or tendencies for perversions; only in connection with the quantitative reinforcement of the significance that they experience do they complete the circle that ascribes to the manifest perversions a special place in metapsychology and technique. This special place derives from the specificity of an instinctual fate in early childhood that leads neither to a psychosis or prepsychosis nor to a narcissistic neurosis, nor to a psychosomatic syndrome or the formation of a psychoneurosis, even though perverse symptoms in all these forms of psychic illness can occur.

What, then, are perversions? A perversion—from a metapsychological point of view—constitutes first and foremost a function. This function can be best described as a sealing plug, a "filling," a heterogeneous formation that closes the gap created by an aberrant narcissistic development. Through this "filling," the homeostasis in the narcissistic area is made possible and maintained.

The term "narcissistic development" is understood as the process that leads to setting the limits of the self. In this process, self-representations and object representations are formed. On the one hand, this happens by means of internalization and integration of the idealized parental imago, whereby the ego-ideal is established. On the other hand, it happens by means of transforming the grandiose self into a pleasurably experienced image of one's own person and body, thus establishing the capability to feel ambitions and to direct them towards goals (Kohut, 1971a). Hereby the feeling of self-value, the relationship with one's own body—in brief, the psychic and sexual identity—is strengthened. From a psychodynamic point of view, the mother's capability to experience appropriate empathy in the dualistic union with the child plays a decisive role. In the healthy process of the narcissistic development, the self fills itself with contents and feelings and rounds itself off. In a disturbed narcissistic development, the integrating and transforming processes have failed; the self does not round itself off—a gap remains. The self becomes empty, void of content, and cold of feeling. Since this is so, the metaphor of a filling, a plug—that is, a connecting or bridging structure—is also suitable for understanding what the function of the development towards a perversion is.

If, in a disturbed narcissistic development, the integrating and reforming processes have failed, it means that the experiences of reality were unable to adapt to the "delusional formations" of the primary-process interpretation of reality. An inner contradiction remains, which continuously threatens and questions the ego structures that have adapted to reality, because illusion and reality cannot be brought into agreement. Perversion as function has the purpose of bridging this inner contradiction and of functionally rounding off and completing the unsuccessful developmental process. Hereby one must further imagine that, while the child is still in the traumatizing period of the narcissistic development, this prosthetic completion is continuously and appositely invented by the child's creative forces in order to fill the horrible gap that the aberrant development of the self threatens to rip open. The prosthetic completion is the result of a transformation of aggressive energies into a polymorphous structure. The more stable this structure, the more it can absorb narcissistic rage. The perverse syndrome thus becomes a fixed part of the entire person; the filling-function of the perversion is durable and solid. If the structure is unstable, aggressive breakthroughs threaten, accompanied by severe regressions. In these cases, the filling-function of the perversion is insufficient.

The stability or instability of the prosthetic bridging structure in the self depends on the further progress of the development of the ego and the libido. In these developmental processes, the prosthetic completion receives its structural and libidinal characteristics, which represent the characteristics of the various clinical forms of sexual perversions. The energies that weld together those conglomerates, which are isolated from the continuous developmental process, are sexuality and aggression. The polymorphous-perverse tendency inherent in human sexuality is quantitatively reinforced by means of nonneutralizable aggression and, in spite of its structural and functional status in the developmental process, is formed into a filling that fits the contour of the gap in the narcissistic sector. Thus, almost artificially, the failing narcissistic development is compensated. The narcissistic development is the foundation upon which ego development and libido development are founded. Adults with a perverse sex life were children whose developments of ego and libido took place on the basis of a narcissistic development with the aid of a filling.

It seems sensible to understand this concept as a series of gradations. Probably, no narcissistic development takes such an ideal course that no filling-formation, remaining more or less silent, would set in. At one end of the scale, we would posit the developments with quiet micro-fillings. On the other end we would find the severely pathological, psychic defect-developments, where the filling-formation fails because the disturbances in the narcissistic area leave such a large gap that repair is out of the question. In the fragmentation that then becomes prominent in the realm of experience, the perverse symptoms appear organized as "links," but separated from other psychic structures. On the whole, one must keep in mind that the great majority of all perverts will be found within the middle ground of this scale. Among these people there will be only a relatively few who will seek medical advice, not to mention undergo psychoanalysis, during the course of their lives. They all have in common, in addition to their conspicuous deviation in their sexual lives, a personality development that allows them to form and maintain libidinally cathected object relationships, and to form and pursue lasting interests; also, their lines of development show no flaw that decisively affects their social realm.

The assumption of such a graded scale also permits emphasizing another point of view. The formation of the filling, which so successfully completes and consolidates, or at least *can* complete and consolidate, a failing narcissistic development in early child-

hood to the extent that the development of ego and libido somehow succeeds—this filling-formation has an inner structure. Within
this structural, intrasystemic order, a new series of gradations can
be recognized. On one end we find the inanimate, unformed, and
undifferentiated object as the core around which the perversion
crystallizes; on the other end we find the animate, well-defined,
highly differentiated object towards which the mature love relationship of the person develops. Here, too, the vast majority of
people will be found in the middle ground of the gradation series.
All forms of homosexuality and bisexuality are found in this
middle ground.

During the course of recent years, I felt a deep scepticism
because I was unable to shake the suspicion that my concept was
no more than an attempt to deal better with my own unconscious
conflicts, reactivated within me during analyses with my patients.
I would not have had the courage to stick uncompromisingly to
this concept had I not experienced a cultural-anthropological confirmation of this concept in Papua, New Guinea. During the great
initiation feast of the Yatmul in the village of Palimbei in the
central Sepik District, I encountered institutionalized transvestism.

The crocodile is the holy animal of this water culture. The
earth on which the village is located is the back of the crocodile,
protruding out of the water. The men's house, the tambaran,
represents it in more condensed form: it is a part of the crocodile's
back, which provides all life and its preservation. In the tambaran
house the young men undergo their initiation. The image of the
scaly hide of the crocodile is cut into their backs and arms through
dozens of deep wounds. Thus the head of the young man coin-
cides with the head of the crocodile, which has great symbolic
significance in the mythology of this head-hunter culture. Once
the healing of the wounds has taken place in the tambaran house,
under severe exclusion of the women, the new initiates return to
the village. A great celebration follows. The initiated are set on
stools and instructed to stare expressionlessly at a place on the
ground. Behind them sit the elders, the fathers, who sing and play
exceptionally sad music. Many of the old men weep. Now the
women of the families of the initiated appear. They are disguised
as men, and they dance, bare-breasted, hectic, phallic, around the
initiated. Sometimes they approach the young men quite closely
and give them little pushes or touch them in an almost tender
manner. The entire village population stands around these groups
in a semicircle. One begins to hear laughter and cries of joy from
the people. A movement goes through all the spectators. In the

distance, one sees peculiar figures limping closer. These are the Wau, the brothers of the initiates' mothers. Grotesquely disguised as women, wearing women's headgear, a type of hood that covers half of the face, they carry in one hand the hardened sago-palm leaf on which the women prepare the food for their families. The Wau fall over, acting helpless and clumsy, and perform all this like some sort of dance. The portrayal of the women's weakness has a cheering effect on everybody because, in the society of the Yatmul, the women are never experienced in such a way. On the contrary, the woman is the center of everything that strengthens and conserves the social unity of the culture.

Now the Wau comes closer. He begins to dance around the initiated and mingles among the women disguised as men. In the meantime the old ones have crawled to their protégés, planted large bunches of palm leaves in front of them into the wet ground, and put a raffia string around the ankles of the initiates. Now they are crouching again among the musicians, the string tightly in hand. The dancing of the disguised women becomes less hectic. Now only a few are still dancing, with gestures of definite fatigue. The people grow very quiet. The sounds of the music and the songs have an indescribable melancholy. The Wau dances around the initiate, now no longer with a helpless but rather touching seduction dance. He kneels in front of him, circles him with tender, stroking movements and a yearning look. Then, suddenly, he runs to the pigpen nearby and rolls, round and round, in the filth. His entire face is smeared with mud. Thus covered he returns. On the palm leaf are bits of pig fodder, which he now takes and tries to stick into the mouth of the initiated, obviously symbolically, but with so much devotion that every spectator gets an uncanny feeling. Uncanny, because with all this happening, the initiated are crouched so completely motionless, staring fixedly at a point in front of them. They—in contrast to all others—do not participate.

It is obvious that the Wau represents the early pregenital mother who accompanies, influences, and jointly decides for her child in all phases of its libido development. In his dance and behavior, he represents the incestual temptation and seduction. The purpose of the whole rite is to demonstrate and portray how the young man, after the completed initiation, is fully incorporated into the male society, that is, the community of the crocodile of the myth, and thus immune to incestuous temptations.

All initiation rites have this purpose. I have experienced many in African cultures. In general, they are full of symbolic meanings, often quite difficult to comprehend. But never before had I seen an initiation rite in which the incestuous temptation and seduction so precisely traced the experiential quality of the early mother–child relationship as with the Yatmul. And in none of the initiation rites known to me is the deep-seated, unconscious connection between the pregenital, phallic mother and the oedipal castration complex so clearly and drastically demonstrated as here: the women disguised as men, who precede the dance of the Wau, are the penisless, phallic women and, simultaneously, the symbol of the castrated father. The Wau, the mother's brother disguised as a woman, represents the phallus, which, even though detached from the woman, belongs to her, and also contains the image of the castrating father hidden beneath the transvestite disguise.

The most touching aspect of this drama is the emotional force with which the occurrence is communicated to and engraved into every single member of the village's community of the crocodile. Not even the stranger can escape this feeling of being moved. Such intensity of exhibitionistic means of expression would never be possible if the actual mother performed the drama. Nor could another woman manage it. In the Yatmul culture, the creative force of the people invented the necessary framework—namely, transvestism—for coping with their needs. One could speak of a sociocultural filling, which can be generally ascribed to all initiation rites, if one considers the integrating effect derived from all these rites an essential point. With the Yatmul people, the transvestism demonstrates this function of the filling particularly clearly when, by means of this common experience, emotional events are so intensively brought into action in the entire society that a consciousness of social identification with this and no other cultural setting arises and continues. Under these circumstances, one is not surprised to see that Christian missions, which in the Sepik River area have an alarming success infiltrating tribes and wreaking cultural destruction, have not been able to gain a foothold in the village of Palimbei, despite many efforts.

Let me now return to my topic and address the position of perversions in the theory of technique. In the analysis of perverse patients, the analyst must respect the perversion's function as a filling in the narcissistic sector. One should avoid in the analytic process three ever-threatening developments:

(1) The transference in these patients must not serve the removal of the filling-function of the sexual syndromes, because there is the threat of a narcissistic regression, caused by the analyst,

which can also damage the successful results of the development of ego and libido.

(2) Since the object cathexes repeatedly produced by the patient in the transference cannot be maintained, there is always the danger that the analyst, as transference object, encourages regressive processes that split up the actual structure of the perverse-symptom formation, thereby exposing the defects in the ego development. In this connection, let me point out the danger of premature interpretation of aggressive stirrings, to which the analyst is especially easily seduced by such patients. When this happens, the perversion loses, so to speak, its inner consistency, and thus its function as a filling. A similar, no less dangerous development may occur in the interpretation process if the analyst one-sidedly represents the societal reality and thus reinforces the intrapsychic polarisation of the analysand.

(3) The perversion as a whole should not be transferred to the person of the analyst, since the fact of being analyzed, or the person of the analyst, can never fulfill the function of the plug — that is, the function of a true filling, or a narcissistic homeostasis. Experience shows that fetishists have a special tendency to proffer such an analytic stalemate. In such cases, an unfavorable, regressive dependency develops in the analytic relationship. The analyst must make sure, and promptly, to detach this proffered transference from his person by interpreting the fantasy character of such ideas and by pointing out the creatively integrating aspect of the transference fantasies.

But what course does the analytic process take with perverted patients? Before I attempt to conceptualize this course, let me give a clinical example. This is the case of an inconspicuous male, 28 years old, with stringy, oily hair, a strained face, a badly fitting suit of the best, but much too heavy, material, and clumsy, richly ornamented shoes. A number of amulets, rings, and pieces of jewelry, discreetly worn, are noted only later. He is a foreigner, working as manager and salesman in a small store belonging to a company in his homeland. He makes sufficient money and lives a lonely life in a small, carefully furnished apartment. His mother lives, in a chronic state of panic, in one of the large European cities. Mini-catastrophes of all kinds, of which she informs him by telephone or by letter, keep the patient in suspense. In his early childhood, he was known to the police stations of that city as the child constantly being lost by his mother. His father, a droll artist, divorced for twenty years, lives on an island. The stepfather is a rough, undistinguished businessman. The patient is a manifest homosexual with a masochistic perversion. He seeks out rough, undistinguished partners, teases them to pursue him, and submits — often under risky circumstances, with ritualized defense acts and in great pain — to anal intercourse, thereby experiencing orgasm. In analysis he told extensively, haltingly, and in a low voice, of his desperation about his sex life, and pointed to the guilt feelings that tortured him because of his indifference towards his mother. I told him I felt he was suffering more from a dreadful sense of emptiness and an inner lack of relationship than from his sexual disturbances. I seemed to understand that, to the contrary, it was precisely the sexual contacts that removed the frightening sense of emptiness, and that he therefore felt a sense of relief even though his sexual experiences were always painful for him.

This interpretation model indicates the decisive point from which one must start in the case of all perversions. Perverse sexual behavior bridges and removes the impossibility, always lurking in the background, to adapt the reality experiences of daily life to the illusionary imaginings of the primary-process interpretation of reality (Lincke, 1981).

The patient was silent for a long time. Tears welled up in his eyes. Finally he expressed his amazement that I had understood him so correctly, even though he was unable to provide me with any kind of clues. Thereupon a transferencelike, idealizing relationship with me began, such as develops in narcissistic neuroses. A deepening of this idealizing relationship took place when I interpreted to him that it was much less his feeling of guilt towards his mother that bothered him than the enormous irritation that he usually felt when he was in contact with me or thinking about me.

These two interpretations became the points of departure for a more and more detailed description of what was going on within him, whereby everything he told me was intended to confirm what I had understood. He loosened up and relaxed during the analytic sessions. Later, I was able to interpret to him how justifiable his attachment to his sexual activities was, since they fulfilled one of the most important functions for him — they put him into a position where he could even begin to be as productive and goal-oriented in life as he was.

A patient with a completely developed narcissistic neurosis would react to such an interpretation with hurt feelings, because he would have to suspect praise or an overestimation of his person, which, owing to his lack of self-esteem, would be unbearable to him. He would say, more or less, that he was neither productive nor goal-oriented and that the analyst no longer understood him at all. Narcissistically disturbed patients react in this manner because with them the split between the illusionary interpretations of reality and the reality of the experience becomes clearly visible.

With my patient, this was different. The revalorization of his sexual symptoms had already contributed to the consolidation of his self-esteem. He now understood my interpretation to mean that he was productive and goal-oriented because of, or by means of, his perversion. And since I seemed to him productive and goal-oriented, he attempted to manipulate me into the role of his illusionary notions of the object. The relationship that up to this point had been floating, transferencelike, dual-unionistic, now suddenly changed into an object-cathected, sado-anal, competitive attitude towards me as a partner. If up to this point I was a mere function that served to complete his self in the sense of an expansion and addition, I now became an object with a specific cathexis. He turned around, looked at me and said: "If you understand everything so well that goes on in me, it can only be because you have the same sexual experiences as I. I assume you accepted me only for treatment because you are homosexual yourself."

He observed me half sadly, half triumphantly. For some time I had expected such a change; it is almost typical for perverted patients. In such an instance, I was prepared to give up my previous role as function, as "expanded self," immediately, and to present myself to the patient as the object of his libidinal cathexis. I told him: "You have talked about your homosexual experiences with only the greatest contempt, and now you are using the notion that I am homosexual in order to give expression to your contempt for me. However, you are only doing this because you are afraid that my understanding for you is no more than lies and deception, and that behind these I am hiding my disdain and contempt for you." Even while I was talking, the patient had lain down again. He was silent.

My interpretation was the correct point of departure, but it was infiltrated by a defense of which I was not aware at that time. My patient's assumption that I had accepted him for treatment because I was homosexual myself doubtlessly complied with his need to interpret in an illusionary way — that is, magically-symbolically — a part of the reality in which he was living now, within the analytic relationship. Although it was already clear to me at that time that this need was not to be refuted by means of the reality experience of the analytic relationship, but that it must be confirmed, anxieties about my own homosexuality had led to the fact that I temporarily ended up in a defense.

The interpretation should have been as follows: "Your fantasy that I have the same sexual experiences as you, and that I am homosexual, expresses how important it is for you to find a partner in me who corresponds to your ideas and who will not refute them. Only if you succeed in this can you feel well. Actually, what you fear is that I would not understand this very need of yours and thus would not really get involved."

In my interpretation, the weight I placed upon contempt was incorrect and motivated by defense. At the same time, it becomes apparent from this example how easily a premature and incorrect interpretation of aggression can occur with perverse patients and homosexuals.

I have already mentioned that my patient kept silent following my interpretation. Then he began: "Incidentally, I wanted to tell you that yesterday evening I drove my car along the quay where you live, looking for a partner. I found one, but lost sight of him later on. Everything had already been arranged. We were to go to my car by separate ways. Then he didn't come. I felt bad, quite empty and useless, as you said. At home it came to my mind that I would have an hour with you again today and that now, after all, I do have you. And I thought that surely you must be perverse, maybe with shoes or leather straps." His voice became softer and softer. He showed a slight motor unrest, twitched his feet, and his hands trembled. He also wiped sweat from his reddened face.

It was apparent that my patient could not maintain the object cathexis he had undertaken with me in the transference. He threatened to regress and to reactivate in me, by projection, the traits of the destructive, preoedipal, phallic mother. Clear signs of irritation indicated this, and that was inadmissible. At such moments the analyst must anticipate that, in order to avoid overtaxing the affective area, he should be active again in the sense of a functional expansion of the patient's self. After all, the perverse patient does not have a structured defense organization available for confronting affective breakthroughs in any other way than with his sexual emergency function, the perversion. From a technical point of view, one must not seek further disclosures at such a point by waiting or questioning. Rather, one has to make sure that the narcissistic form of the earlier, transferencelike relationship becomes reestablished. I therefore did not hesitate to provide the patient with a reconstructive interpretation that traced the actualized transference reference back to his early childhood fate. In doing so, I tried to formulate what I had guessed from his descriptions during previous sessions. It is an important experience to learn that it is particularly the reconstructive interpretation, which is based much more on an empathic understanding than on verbalized memories, that is technically well suited to further an idealizing form of narcissistic transference.

Therefore I told the patient: "I can understand very well what happened inside you yesterday, after you lost your sadistic homosexual partner and when, at home, you were thinking about your analytic sessions and me. You were actually moved by me, my understanding, and my caring. But you did not know what to do with your being moved. It was foreign to you. This is how once, in your childhood, your mother felt towards you, a touching little boy whom she did not know what to do with, who remained alien to her. Your mother panicked when she lost you in the street or the department store. This panic was the expression of an irritation she felt instead of the warm, tender feelings of caring, which were closed to her."

My patient relaxed, stopped trembling, and seemed to have calmed down. I continued: "Actually, it is not at all true what I said about contempt. What you have contempt for is at most your inability to sense another's caring and to enjoy your own caring. You despise neither me nor your homosexuality; on the contrary, you are full of hope to feel comfortable both here and with your homosexual partners."

After this interpretation, with which I was able, intuitively and without consciously having understood it, to give up my defense in the countertransference, my patient was overwhelmed by the emotions within him. The idealization I experienced was soon boundless and expressed itself in a striking change. He looked much better, often had a radiant quality about his expression, and became active and full of enterprise. A bit of autoplastic adaptation, instead of the previous alloplasty, had occurred. He visited bars and restaurants where homosexuals congregated and for the first time in his life found a gentle partner with whom he was able to enjoy homosexual love.

Much later he met a much younger partner. They laughed and joked and arranged a night of love. But then they talked for hours until the conversation turned into a psychoanalytic situation in which the younger one described his problems and conflicts, my patient provided finely differentiated answers, even interpretations, and finally both fell asleep next to each other, exhausted, shortly before dawn. The sexual contact seemed, without any conflict, to have become superfluous to both. These remarks must suffice as illustrations for illuminating the concept of the theory of technique I shall now briefly summarize.

The lines according to which the analytic process develops follow the laws of the dynamics and the economy of cathexis of the filling's function within the narcissistic area of experience, that is, that function which decisively affects the sexual behavior. What it this function?

Perverted persons cathect their objects and the actions of their partners—and homosexuals, their partners as total persons—with libido on a trial basis. This libidinal cathexis is taken over by the partner in the form of an identification or used as a fusion in order to charge the self-representations (Greenacre, 1955). Since the leading object loses its cathexis at the precise moment when the self should be cathected, the self remains empty. The reason for this is that the self and the object are not sufficiently separated. The insufficient separation of self and object causes bewilderment and contradiction between fantasy and reality.

This mode of cathexis is made quantitatively and qualitatively more dramatic by sexuality. Quantitatively, in that the cathexis modality begins to oscillate between self and object and is heightened by sexual excitation. At the moment of orgasm, a sudden quantitative change occurs, in that sexual gratification, transformed into a sense of well-being, provides the self and the object with strengthened exponents. Such stabilization of exponents—no matter how little durability they may have—takes place even when the fantasy is only temporarily lent the character of reality. A narcissistic equilibrium is established. If now, under the pressure of reality, a narcissistic disharmony threatens to reoccur, the condition of urgency that leads to perverse acts is automatically established.

The analyses of such patients usually begin with tentative libidinal cathexes of the analyst as object. A transference occurs, as with the psychoneuroses. What differentiates the former from the latter is an often violent, but always premature, sexualization, whereby the transference may disintegrate dangerously by means of regression, because the experience threatens to refute the fantasy. Usually, severe regressions occur less frequently than do negative therapeutic reactions. The patient no longer lets himself be involved; the analysis breaks off. The premature sexualization can be recognized by the irritating tensions in the transference, which can quickly be pacified if the analyst concurs with the readiness of the patient to permit and built up a narcissistic, idealizing, or mirroring transference. This readiness is present because the libidinal object cathexis, according to the model of the filling-function of the perversion, must be guided to the self. If this transformation of the transference succeeds, the analyst stops being an object. He is now a function in the service of the "expanded self" (Kohut, 1971a). Since the cathexis of the object is continuously transformed into a cathexis of the self, the analytic process takes place; that is, a new formulation of the perversion occurs. The model of the transformation of the perversion in the analytic process is a concept of the theory of technique and can be paraphrased more clearly from two points of view.

One aspect concerns events in the transference. What has been offered during the phase of the object cathexis with regard to transference contents is integrated into the subsequent phase of the narcissistic expansion of the self. Through this, the self-representatives are strengthened and the individualization process furthered. Then follows a new phase of object cathexis with specific transference contents, which again is followed by a phase of narcissistic expansion. In this process of change, the narcissistic wound, which originated in early childhood, heals under the protection of the intact filling, that is, by the conservation of the perversion as such.

The other aspect is a functional one and refers to the contents of imagination. The primary-process interpretation of reality, deeply seated in the unconscious, has illusionary character in every person. In perversions, a particularly distinctive polarization between the illusionary interpretation of reality, on the one side, and the experience of reality, on the other, has set in. This leads to an inner contradiction, which is resolved by means of the perverse sexual life. In the analytic process, the perversion undergoes a transformation, to the extent that, in the interpretation process, the reality experience of the analytic relationship is brought into harmony with the illusionary ideas of the analysand. This transformation occurs part consciously, part unconsciously. In the phases of object cathexis of the transference, the polar opposites between reality and illusion are aggravated. The interpretation work brings these contrasts into the conscious. In the phases of narcissistic expansion, these diverging structures become integrated. This process is unconscious. It corresponds to a process of introjection, which initiates the healing process of the perversion—this is similarly valid for homosexuality and for bisexual relationships.

Here we have the possibility of a significant misunderstanding, determined by socio-economic, that is, societal processes. If the analyst expects the healing process to consist in having the perversion, homosexuality, and bisexuality all disappear or mitigate in order to be replaced by "normal" heterosexual sex objects, he unconsciously follows the social role assigned to him by society. The healing process does not consist of having something or other disappear. Rather, it consists of the fact that a genuine love relationship is formed, free of conflict, and pleasurable, under the robe of the perverse structure. That is something very remarkable and peculiar, and at first difficult to empathize with if the perverse patient deals with inanimate objects. The most important aspect in this occurrence is the analysand's newly gained capability to bring the illusion into congruence with reality. After a while, the whole matter takes on the characteristics of happy dealings with objects during play. It is extraordinarily impressive to experience how the perversion heals into a game of love.

If the analytic process has progressed to that extent, the narcissistic gap is closed and the filling-function of the perversion has become flexible. It can be removed like a bandage that protected a wound that has now healed underneath. Yet, only the analysand can try the removing. He attempts it autonomously, driven by his sexual curiosity. He will try it tentatively and will constantly refer back to the bandage's function as a filling—for the rest of his life.

Where that will lead, and to what extent the maturization of the sex life can progress, are questions beyond the analytic goal. As in all analyses with psychoneuroses, scars will remain here, too, which do not need to be removed in order to safeguard mental health. There are societal criteria, socio-economic compulsions, that force us all into the achievement principle. Out of this point of view arose the demand that one eliminate perversions and their derivatives before one dared define or terminate an analysis as successful. The questions arising in this connection often lead to misunderstandings. Basically it is a question of whether the successful transference structures of the analytic process correspond to those which society regards as being "normal." The contradictions that appear, particularly in this comparison, are of great significance for the theory of technique because they influence the perception and the attitude of the analyst to a greater extent than is usually thought. When we formulate concepts in the theory of technique, these concepts must be brought into connection with the technique of interpretation in order to find points of reference for the practical analytic work. The technique of interpretation orients itself fundamentally on the basis of the dynamics of transference and the defense processes.

In the analytic process with perverse patients, the dynamics of transference play a very special part. An erotization of the transference is present if there is a quick change of transferential forms of the object-directed libido cathexis, on the one hand and of the narcissistic form of the relationship, on the other. That erotization leads to a regression of the analytic relationship to a sado-anal level and can be recognized by a tension-filled role-playing between analyst and analysand. The patient, following his fantasies, attempts to manipulate the analyst, who defends himself against it. A contest situation develops which is difficult to comprehend and which blocks the analysis.

The evaluation of the defense processes is usually decisive for the course of the analysis. The patients of interest to us here always manifest an unstable defense organization. The defense is insufficient owing to the quantitative reinforcement of the affect quota in the object relationships. If our patients enter into narcissistically expanding relationships, the defense organization is almost completely missing. These defense functions must be built up fundamentally in the analysis. If resistances become perceptible, they are mostly directed against regressive processes. They must not be interpreted as defenses, because doing so will only lead to unbearable tensions and irritations. What appears as resistance in the analytic process is, rather, a signal for the reorientation of the transference.

In a longitudinal view of the analytic course, we can, from the viewpoint of the theory of technique, describe a gradually emerging and necessary restructuring of the transference dynamics, which probably will be of decisive importance in the analysis of perversions. From the metapsychological point of view, this is most likely a matter of intrasystemic processes that initiate the terminal phase of the analysis. In my opinion, however, these events can be described better by means of transference events than theoretically.

As the analysis progresses, the analyst gets to know his analysand better and better and increases his capability to foresee the imminent changes of one form of transference into another in an ever more differentiated way. From then on, the analytic process can undergo changes that open new aspects, and the process intensifies. This does not happen all by itself. The analyst must take on a new task. By foreseeing the imminent restructuring of the transference, he must adjust his attitude towards the analysand: now in anticipation of the object cathexis of his person, then again in anticipation of the narcissistic need of his patient to experience the analyst in the function of his, the patient's, own expanded self. Thus the analyst accepts the back-and-forth of an intrapsychic reorientation into which the patient has been forced again and again by fear. This restructuring in the transference dynamics is crucial for the success of the analytic process. The analysand gradually develops a constant relationship with his analyst, which follows a straight line, and in which the autonomous functions are more and more guaranteed.

This development leads to the point where the analysand structures his object relationships in such a manner that they correspond to his unconscious oedipal fantasies. For long stretches of the analytic process with perverse patients, the oedipal conflicts and castration fears appear in mystically distorted form and thus cannot be designated as oedipal according to our definition. To the extent that the initial primary-process contents of ideas are transformed into more mature forms of reality interpretations, and to the extent that these contents can be integrated by means of genuine experiences in the analytic relationship, the entire complex of symbolic correlations of meanings gradually approaches the language and the forms of expression of our society. This then permits the connection of the perverse images to the nearly realistic conflict constellation of the oedipal situation. Not until the integration process has greatly progressed—in the final phase of the analytic process—will the analysand adapt to the socially and culturally prescribed level of society where we can feel empathy for the oedipal reality, and comprehend it. Then the connection prevailing in perversions between the cathexis economy and the oedipal constellation will also become clearer. For if the analyst has succeeded in accepting the back-and-forth of the intrapsychic reorientation of the transference, it will come to pass during the further course of the analysis that the analysand's castration anxieties will be neutralized in the transference. One is justified in assuming this, because it is only then that the analysand brings to light the crucial link between his perversion and the oedipal conflicts.

3

PSYCHOANALYTIC TECHNIQUE IN THE TREATMENT OF NEUROTIC HOMOSEXUALS

Fundamentally, psychoanalytic research is not happy with the problem of homosexuality. With a phobia, a hysterical character neurosis, or a compulsion symptom, it does not encounter the same problems as with homosexuality. Homosexual tendencies, in sublimated form, generally serve the process of social adaptation and the getting along with the partner of the same sex. In that regard the psychoanalysts's way of life is of no particular concern. If analysts themselves have been thoroughly analyzed, they know in what areas of their development homosexual tendencies and attachments cannot be dismissed, because these tendencies served as a bridge that made it possible to get along with friends, relatives, and colleagues of the same sex. Such tendencies, perhaps in finely-spun, sublimated forms, have during the course of their lives provided the analysts with gratifications that they would not want to relinquish.

Whereas public opinion in general confronts homosexuality with hostility, psychoanalysts are more tolerant. They want to investigate, comprehend, and explain the background of homosexuality without prejudice. However, analysts, as a part of the society they live in, can maintain this tolerance with regard to homosexuality only to a certain degree. Almost all of the numerous aspects being discussed today in psychoanalytic research on homosexuality contain the demand, overt or covert, to undertake something drastic against this "evil." After neither laws nor punishment, neither education nor religion have been able to counter this expression of "human depravity," successfully, psychoanalysis raises its voice and enters the fray in the service of society. It seems as if many psychoanalysts use a different yardstick in the treatment of homosexuals than with other psychic "disturbances." In the psychoanalytic treatment of manifest homosexuals, analysts are easily seduced into wanting to decide the manner in which their analysands will finally live and love.

As obvious as it is for all analysts that one cannot reconcile such aims with the analytic task, it nevertheless seems justifiable to them in the treatment of homosexuals to aim for a specific form of love life. In this they fall prey to a deception, for analytic treatment pursues an entirely different goal. It sets itself the task of alleviating repressions that lead to symptoms. If technique is emphasized, one knows how significant it is for the development of transference and countertransference that analysts not let themselves get involved in the struggle against a symptom. They will interpret resistances in the light of expressions of transference. Then, usually, the symptom disappears. The fact that psychoanalysts always want to cure homosexuals hides an emotional stirring in the analyst's unconscious that can easily fall prey to unnoticed defenses. It is a peculiar fact that in the course of an analysis, analysts can deal much more easily with transferences with heterosexual overtones than they can with homosexual transferences. During the analysis of a homosexual problem, analysts are threatened by their unconscious with the reactivation of their own homosexual tendencies. With regard to the analyst, the countertransference in analyses with homosexuals is exposed to particular stresses, whereas homosexual analysands have a tendency to influence the analyst's countertransference, by unconscious means, to such an extent that the analytic process is disturbed. In my experience this applies primarily to analysands with indications of manifest homosexuality. However, the same difficulty can arise with latently homosexual patients.

In the following section, I will focus on the consequences of the strain on countertransference in analyses with neurotic homosexuals, investigating them from the point of view of analytic technique. Theoretical references will be secondary in that regard and will be discussed only insofar as they are necessary for practical purposes of the analytic treatment.

As is known, psychoanalysis deduced the origin of homosexuality from the oedipal conflict. At the same time, it never differentiated between neurotic homosexuality and a nonneurotic development into homosexuality. For this reason, the problems arising during the treatment of homosexual analysands were not satisfactorily solved by the resulting findings. In the course of time, a confusing array of views regarding the possible background of homosexuality emerged, whereby, however, little attention was given to the question why analysis with homosexuals is continuously exposed to severe disturbances. On the one hand, the increasing indifference regarding the Oedipus complex led to the result that the theoretical aspects of inversion became more and more complex and confused. On the other hand, the ever greater significance that the observation of pregenital disturbances is assuming in the theory of neurosis in general has resulted in the fact that the technique of analytic treatment of homosexuals has been affected to its disadvantage. From a theoretic point of view there may have been much definite proof that severe pregenital disturbances are the actual reason for neurotic homosexuality; however, one should not overlook the fact that it is only the characteristic formation of the Oedipus complex that brings about the actual symptomatology of neurotic homosexuality. If this point of view is not kept in mind in practical analytic work with homosexuals, the danger exists that the analyst may underestimate the decisive defense mechanisms that the homosexual analysand expresses in the transference. The analyst will erroneously or prematurely address the pregenital traits of the patient without having sufficiently considered the oedipal problems. To make clear what I mean here, the oedipal problems of neurotic homosexuals must be briefly reconsidered: male, and probably also female, homosexuality is a matter of the final condition of a complex development based on an attachment to the mother, with whom the homosexual identifies. The neurotic homosexual male loves his object the way he wishes his mother had loved him. In his own person, he denies his mother's lack of a penis and cannot tolerate the missing penis in the beloved object because of the threatening castration anxiety.

From these circumstances, brought to light in the analysis of such neurotic homosexual males, psychoanalysis believed it recognized that castration anxiety had to be responsible for the inversion of the sexual object. It seems that at the peak of the oedipal conflict, some form of admittedly unusual repression of the incestual desire occurs, which subsequently results in the identification with the mother. In this connection, one has to assume that the incestual wish is originally countered by the paternal threat of castration and warded off by a flight from the mother (possibly also from the sister), and that it is this event that eventually causes the castration anxiety to become connected with the mother.

From that point on, the absence of a penis in the female would have to trigger the castration anxiety. It thus becomes understandable that an identification with the mother is capable of banning the castration anxiety, since the homosexual who takes the place of the mother can, with the help of his own person, continuously disavow the absence of a penis. This result of the repression of the incestual wish causes a regression to the *phallic-narcissistic* stage of instinctual development, for the narcissistic overestimation of the own person as the "penis bearer" is the necessary safeguard against the return of what was repressed.

There is a form of homosexuality in which the identification with the mother has another fate. The homosexual, like the mother, expects to be penetrated by the father; he disavows his masculinity to his father and turns his back to him. This homosexual submits passively to his partner, who has anal intercourse with him. Seen from a psychoanalytic point of view, the fate of this incestual wish corresponds to the negative outcome of the oedipal conflict and, as experience shows, will result in a regression to the *sado-anal* stage of instinctual development.

The neurotic lesbian loves her girl friend the way she wishes her mother had loved her. The fantasized wish fulfillment to be a boy is thereby emphasized. As with the man, there is the other outcome of the identification with the mother. The lesbian loves in her friend the fantasized masculine properties of her father in the way she wishes for her mother to love him. The lesbian cathects the phantasized penis of the friend, or her love for her own phantasized penis, and loathes the male phallus, for which she feels fear and revulsion. Direct contact with a man results in the breakthrough of manifest incestual wishes.

When observing the psychoeconomic relationships of the libido cathexes, no basic difference is apparent between male and female neurotic homosexuality. The male cathects the real penis, the female the penis fantasy. Just as the male in his identification disavows the absence of a penis in the mother, the female disavows the absence of her own penis. The male must find the penis in his beloved object in order to evade castration anxiety, whereas the female rejects it in order to secure further the repression of the incestual desire.

The confusion that had resulted from the terms active, passive, feminine, and masculine was cleared up only after active and passive tendencies, masculine and feminine traits could be demonstrated in every homosexual. It was recognized that homosexuals could take either the one or the other attitude in their relationships with the same partner, even within the same hour of their being together. From this we can conclude that phallic-narcissistic as well as sado-anal fixations are probably existent in all cases of homosexuality, but that in any given case, either one or the other of the fixations can be recognized particularly clearly in the development of character.

In deducing the origin of neurotic homosexuality from the Oedipus complex, we have by no means explained what the preconditions are for the oedipal conflict to take this unusual course. In the pursuit of this question, psychoanalytic research has made the assumption of a fixation connected with a disturbance in the mother–child relationship during the oral phase. At this point it would seem reasonable to go into the theories dealing with the problems of ego formation. I will have to refrain from this here, since our focus is not on the theory of homosexuality but rather on the various points of view with regard to technique in the treatment of homosexuals.

One theoretical point of view, however, should be mentioned in this connection because it is significant for the practical application of the analysis: it is the often assumed unstable and weak ego structure of the homosexual, which is compared in many ways with the ego structure of prepsychotic patients. Although many theoretical considerations support such an assumption, the aspect that seems much more important to me is that, especially with homosexuals, there is generally no prepsychotic or near-psychotic state apparent. Rather, the entire defense hidden in the neurotic homosexuality is directed towards a threatening oral regression. Indeed, the whole point of this form of homosexuality is to prevent such a regression by all possible means, even though it seems indispensable for unconscious wish fulfillment and sexual gratification. In other words, in the further course of the development to the point of manifest homosexuality, the legacies of the Oedipus complex—that is, the regressively cathected phallic-narcissistic and sado-anal fixation points—mainly serve as defense against a development towards a clinically ascertainable pregenital neurosis. With the neurotic homosexual, the entire oedipal problem represents a complex stronghold of defense, rather insidious for the analyst, which is supposed to protect the analysand from his actual problem, his deepest anxiety, namely, from the threatening oral regression. As far as the method of the psychoanalytic treatment is concerned, there can be no doubt that with homosexuality the analysis can only progress by consistently dealing with the phallic-narcissistic and sado-anal tendencies.

Neurotic homosexuality can be termed a regressive adaptation that prevents an oral regression. It serves the defense and is the expression of the repression of the Oedipus complex. The incest wish and castration anxiety provoke a regression that rests on two fixation points—one is sado-anal; the other, phallic-narcissistic. The castration anxiety chases the homosexual from one level of regression to the other, while the incest wish finds gratification in either one or the other libido position. The two libido positions, the sado-anal and the phallic-narcissistic, can be interchanged with the greatest ease. The homosexual fixation is found in this double track of the regression procedure. The homosexual cannot do without it, because of the threat of a further regression. This regression to oral fixations would lead to a complete dissolution and disintegration of the ego.

The regressive adaptation would have two aims: to repress the Oedipus complex, thus evading it, and yet to escape the threatening oral regression. The advantages this form of regressive adaptation provides are of extraordinary significance.

(1) The original oral fixations on the mother, which determine the fate of every libidinal gratification in the neurotic homosexual, are still taken into account. The incestual desire is unconsciously retained. This type of homosexual uses the orgastic experience of mature sexuality in order to reexperience the demands for oral dependence in his fantasy, and he succeeds. The renunciation of the primary attainment of pleasure with the original object is thus rendered unnecessary.

(2) The necessity to expand an object relationship and to hold on to it is absent in such homosexuals, because they cultivate the double-tracked regressive form of adaptation, in which they can continuously exchange the libido position with the same partner. One gets the impression that the main aspect of the attainment of pleasure these homosexuals seek and find is based precisely on this exchangeability of the phallic-narcissistic and the sado-anal cathexis.

(3) Neurotic homosexuals fear libidinal excitations because such excitations menacingly advance oral regression into the foreground. In their safety apparatus—the two-level regression—they escape from one libido cathexis into the other whenever they feel threatened internally or externally by libidinal excitation.

(4) Finally, the system offers them the opportunity to remain faithful to their tendency to enter into merely temporary identifications. This faithfulness is directed towards the oral mother. Frequently they renounce the durability of an object relationship.

The presence of the homosexual partner is more important for the pleasurable erotic play within the regressive acting out than is the partner's significance as a love object. Gratification occurs primarily in the fantasy.

If homosexuality is viewed in this manner, it becomes comparable with the head of Janus, only one of whose two faces is ever visible at one time. The other one is sought by the homosexual in his or her partner, whose characteristics correspond to those libido cathexes which the homosexual does not engage in at the moment, but to which he or she can revert in a playful manner, just as the partner does in reciprocation. These characteristics of the partner are more important than the total person. The libido follows the satisfaction of the need, not the type of support. The entire intensity of *infantile sexual curiosity* is directed, in part consciously, in part unconsciously, towards these characteristics sought in the partner. Its aim is to find in the partner the ability to be seduced. Homosexuals are elementally curious to experience, or to fantasize, to what degree their partners will provide the prerequisites they themselves have, in order that the tender and sensual wishes may attain the expected gratification.

In a neurotic development to homosexuality, one can speak of a regressive adaptation in which the two levels of regression are always cathected in such a manner that one level is being experienced, whereas the other is projected onto the partner and is thereby mirrored back. The entire process is an imitation of heterosexual love, a regressive unit of reaction that permits the interplay of sexual passions and, like no other form of neurotic fixation and symptom formation, promises possibilities of gratification most closely associated with those of the heterosexual ability to love. In general, homosexual gratification is much closer to heterosexual gratification than to any form of perverse attainment of pleasure. Nonneurotic homosexuals can be just as fully involved in their love as any nonneurotic, sexually mature persons. The most sublime forms of tender and sensual aspirations can develop within this love.

For the most part, we do not find in the homosexual inclination any signs of an actual inability to love, that is, if neurotic moments do not aggravate the circumstances. Severe guilt feelings, contact disturbances, inhibitions of all kinds, self-accusations, and aggressive outbreaks are found as frequently in disturbed heterosexual relationships as in neurotic homosexuals.

The analytic experience in the treatment of neurotic homosexuals permits one to assume that gratification, as previously mentioned, is much more connected to the exchangeability of the phallic-narcissistic and sado-anal cathexis than to the love relationship with the partner. But how can it be explained that it is this very change from one regressive position to another that leads to so elementary a sensation of pleasure, which can attain the most sublime expression of tender and sensual aspirations? I can provide no such explanation. One observation from an analysis with a nonhomosexual analysand, however, has allowed me to surmise how the dynamic relationships might occasionally be comprehended.

A few weeks before the termination of a long, well-advanced working-through of passive, subservient traits that were apparent in the relationship of a patient with his father and transferred onto the analyst, the secret fear of the violent father figure, who would jealously interfere with a satisfying heterosexual relationship of the patient, was still noticeable. He continuously got into arguments with his wife and subserviently reported these frictions, full of reproaches towards his wife, during the analysis. After an interpretation of his anxiety and a working through of the compulsion to repeat that he expressed in his behavior, the arguing suddenly stopped and the patient was able to enjoy a happy relationship with his wife. When he proudly reported this in the analysis, he provided me with the occasion to interpret the positive feelings he had for his father. I told him at the same time that he secretly had similar feelings of attachment in his analytic relationship. This ability to love, I continued, was now cathected by him for the first time in the sense of a healthy narcissism. He sensed his own security and peace because now he was in unthreatened possession of his genital ability to love. At this point the patient was overcome by a peculiar feeling of emotion, a feeling of longing such as he had never before experienced, which made him weep quietly. He did not understand where this emotion came from. The emotional excitation was the expression of his earlier relationship with his mother, an emotional aftereffect of previously overcome incestual wishes.

The sado-anal fixation on the father had been converted into the narcissistic enjoyment of an unthreatened ability to love. During this process, evidently, very early oral strivings were activated, which, in the form of sadness, were mixed into the narcissistic self-admiration of his own genitals, whereby it was precisely the phallic-narcissistic cathexis that could be relinquished in favor of the object relationship with the heterosexually loved wife. In this analysis, the transition of a sado-anal striving into a narcissistic one was the outcome of much analytic work, and, as a consequence of overcoming the oedipal conflicts, it resulted in the introjection of the father, whereby the activation of very early, probably oral stirrings awakened memories of the bodily presence of the mother. The sadness admixed with this emotion was the expression of the renunciation of the mother that accompanied the introjection process. This process represented the bridge to a genital love relationship.

With neurotic homosexuals, one can assume that the same process as a whole is fixated in a reaction formation. Here, too, a forced leap from an anal-sadistic to a phallic-narcissistic mode of experience will provoke oral stirrings, which are reminders of the incestual wish but do not lead to renunciation. No emotional stirring results, but rather a strong erotization. In the playful alternation from one regressive cathexis to another, the homosexual can escape the effects of the incestual wish, can avoid castration anxiety, and, by means of the inversion of the sexual object, present the plagiarism of a matured ability to love. It must remain plagiarism, because the Oedipus complex is continuously effective. In an endless sequence, a sado-anal regression is provoked, particularly when the admixture of oral stirrings in the phallic-narcissistic cathexis of the patient's own genitality forms the bridge to castration anxiety. With nonneurotic homosexuals this is not the case.

The double-tracked regressive fixation provides neurotic homosexuals with great flexibility and relative stability in their relationship to their environment. In it they find the actual gain from their illness, which regularly dominates in analysis in the form of a resistance. The gratification they attain in their sexual relationships with their partners, in its role as the cause of this gain, is moved into the background. In reality, the sexual gratification of the neurotic homosexual is no greater than the gratification of a heterosexual person whose ability to enjoy is restricted by emotional disturbances.

From this point of view, the defining of homosexuality according to phallic-narcissistic and anal-sadistic groupings is no more than a phenomenological structuring. All homosexuals show phallic-narcissistic as well as anal-sadistic tendencies. They outwardly display, and consciously sense, only the traits of one of the two faces of the homosexual head of Janus. In every libidinal cathexis from outside, or by means of a libidinal nudge from within, homosexuals can, amazingly, and relatively effortlessly, take on the traits of the second face.

Psychoanalytic treatment with a manifest homosexual is particularly well suited to reflect these circumstances, because the libidinal cathexes are ordered in a very precise manner during the formation of the transference. It is here, in these cathexes, that the analytic process takes place. The fate of the transference determines the forms of resistance and the effect of interpretations. In the transference, the homosexual feels prematurely overtaxed. The handling of the transference in the analysis of homosexuals is therefore the most important factor of psychoanalytic technique.

In the analysis of neurotic homosexuals, the aim is to permit the formation of the violently warded-off *oral regression* within the development of transference and thereby to break through the sado-anal and phallic-narcissistic fixations. In so doing, psychoanalytic technique follows two principles, the general validity of which is well known: (1) The acting out of the patient is to be reduced by interpretation of behavior and by conversion into recall. (2) The significance and the meaning of homosexuality are to be clarified.

As far as the *acting out* of the homosexual is concerned, psychoanalysis errs when it postulates that this is first of all a matter of clinically evident homosexual activity. When faced with homosexuality, analysts are in the difficult situation of having to ignore, for the moment, the actual homosexual symptomatology in their analytic work and to completely address themselves to the background of the fixations that condition it. Here, the overestimated question of the analyst's sex is unimportant.

In order to eventually master the acting out of the homosexual analysand, two points of view, among many, regarding technique should be particularly emphasized.

(1) Psychoanalytic technique must particularly observe the two-sidedness of the homosexuals' behavior and must detect it, recognize it, and interpret it everywhere: in the patient's attitudes, remarks, gestures, in self-judgment, fantasies, wishes, and in the association material reported by the patient. Here is a brief example:

An analysand with latent or manifest neurotic homosexual tendencies, whether male or female, whether with a male or female analyst, demonstrates, for example, a very remarkable characteristic with regard to self-judgment. If the analysand assumes a passive-submissive attitude and is full of declared confidence regarding the analyst and the treatment, he or she often shows a definite narcissistic trait in self-judgment. The patient rejects practically all interpretations of his or her behavior. All analysts know such situations from their own practice. They know how hard the struggle can be, insofar as one provides the opportunity for it.

As a prototype of an interpretation, one might use the following: "You are so noticeably obliging in all matters, so amiable. Only when I try to tell you something do you become reticent and rejecting." However, if analysts attempt to interpret the narcissistically conditioned rejection as if they did not notice the subservient attitude of the patient, saying, for instance, "You cannot accept what you are told because you are so defiant," they accept the struggle to which the analysand wants to seduce them.

Such a struggle is consciously or unconsciously experienced by homosexual analysands as a courtship with intent to seduce. These analysands feel as if their analysts wanted to rape them from behind with their interpretation. Since the patients miss the desired erotic attainment of pleasure in this situation, they seek, after a while, the longed-for substitute outside analysis, in their fantasies or with homosexual contacts. In these fantasies the analyst becomes the unsuccessful seducer who is not homosexual enough to please the analysand. If the struggling situation becomes sufficiently erotized, and if the analysands thus feel threatened, they begin acting out in a phallic-narcissistic manner. Thanks to the noticeable exhibitions and impressive gestures, the intention to seduce is much more superficial and clearly recognizable. The interpretations are now accepted subserviently and commented upon. However, the goal remains the seduction, through which the analysands want to give their analysts occasion to reveal themselves, to expose their intentions, feelings, and opinions. The patients experience the inadequacy of their analyst, who cannot measure up to their loving homosexual desires, and they turn away disappointed. They find themselves another partner as a substitute. In the patient's fantasies the analyst becomes a partner who wanted to do everything to be considered as a homosexual love object, but who did not succeed because the proffered means were not sufficiently attractive and thus of little use to the patient.

(2) The second point of view to be emphasized with regard to the governability of neurotic homosexuals' acting out concerns the infantile sexual curiosity with which the homosexual analysand would like to explore the analyst's spiritual impulses, fantasies, and sex life. This tendency is sometimes quite apparent, at other times very much hidden and hardly perceptible.

When neurotic homosexuals ask the analyst whether they are curable or not, the question contains a seduction. It is a trick question to which the homosexual will cling stubbornly. Psychoanalysts have a tendency, in their answers to patients, in publications, and in entire congressional symposia, to identify themselves with this question. When analysands would like to force the analyst to take a position on this question, it becomes apparent from the behavior of these neurotic homosexuals how much, on the one hand, they wish their homosexuality were curable and, on the other hand, how much deep distrust, anticipatory fear, and disappointment lie ready within them, should the prospect of a cure be presented as a definite possibility. It is clear that this question from the analysand contains only one item: the curiosity to know what the analyst's emotions and feelings are. This curiosity on the part of the neurotic homosexual permits us to recognize the infantile sexual curiosity in its original intensity almost in its pure form. In any event, analysts find themselves in a difficult situation, whether they are aware of this problem or must suppress it and compensate for it with a conventualized attitude. Wherever homosexual tendencies become apparent in the human psyche and express themselves in transference, we are almost always dealing with infantile sexual curiosity and the intention to seduce. The dangers that threaten the analysis of homosexuals at such moments are general in nature and occur especially easily whenever some insufficiently analyzed, unresolved problem in the inner life of the analyst is touched upon by way of the patient's unconscious. The following is a brief example from a supervisory situation, which at first glance seems to have nothing to do with homosexuality as such.

Some time ago, a middle-aged spinster in a very agitated state sought my advice. For many years, she had been occupied with educational counseling and child analysis. She was very gifted and successful, but even her own analysis had not succeeded in giving her fate a different direction, and so she remained virginal, unmarried, but was fairly satisfied with her life. She was treating an eight-year-old boy who had so fallen prey to daydreams that he was no longer able to follow instruction in school. He told her about his travels to the moon, where he visited all the moon animals, which he described and drew in detail. Her sessions with this boy led to an astounding success. The boy worked to the satisfaction of his school teacher and proved to be much livelier and more active also at home. Then suddenly the boy came with a demand which he continued to pose more and more aggressively. He wanted to know what was happening when the bull mounted the cow. The therapist attempted to talk reasonably to the boy and to provide him with an answer appropriate to his age. The boy, however, was dissatisfied and disappointed. Then he threatened,

"If you don't tell me what happens when the bull mounts the cow, I shall ask the gardener and the farmer; then I shall ask the teacher and the people on the street." The elderly spinster found herself in distress. What should she do? She decided to explain to the boy the sexual act between animals, and was driven by the boy's demand to reveal ever more and more details. But the boy remained dissatisfied and defiant. He left the therapist with these words: "If you don't want to tell me anything, I shall ask my father and my mother." The lady detained the boy and interpreted for him his wish, namely, to know more exact details about the sexual intercourse of his parents. The boy replied that he knew all about that; he had spoken with his pals and also asked his parents. The gardener had also explained to him what happens when the bull mounts the cow. The agitated therapist came to see me because after this session she spent a sleepless night and began suffering states of anxiety. I interpreted for her that the boy, with his demand for sexual enlightment, wanted primarily to know about her own sexuality. In the transference, the sexual curiosity of early childhood became directed at the therapist. Since she could not have had any experience in sexual matters herself, she found herself in conflict in the face of this new aspect of the transference.

This brief case description has nothing to do with homosexuality. However, it points out the problematical situation into which a homosexual might lead the analyst, perhaps in a much more mitigated form. In undertaking to analyze a homosexual, the analyst must not be led into the position of the elderly spinster, whose curious boy got her into a confusion of good intentions and desperate defense, to the point where she was able neither to see nor interpret his curiosity about her own sexual behavior. One's personal attitude and opinion about homosexuality should not be laid bare. In so doing, one would yield to the seduction inherent in the curiosity.

Let a brief example demonstrate how the coacting out of the therapist may be provoked and avoided during the initiation of the analysis of a neurotic homosexual patient.

A pale, timid young man was brought to my office by his father. His father immediately asked me whether homosexuality was curable. He did not wait for an answer, but added that he begged me to take his son into analysis if I could give a positive answer to his question. "What do you think about it?" was my counter question, this time directed at the son. The young man contorted his limbs, looked at the floor and said nothing. "He is shy and full of a bad conscience," the father continued, "but I am in the way here. He won't talk to you until you are alone with him." The father stood up and took his leave. I asked the son to take a seat, in the chair in which his father had sat, and began to talk: "Your father must not have felt at ease, he left so suddenly." "He was afraid of you," was the answer.

In the first ten minutes, father and son provoked the analyst with a series of trick questions and statements. The doctor was supposed to reveal himself, divulge his opinions. He was to involve himself immediately, hold back the father, and provide sensible explanations. He was to be ready to identify with persons and problems. The son attempted to arouse the doctor's curiosity. His first sentence was, "My father is afraid of you." I was supposed to ask why, to have been disconcerted, or to have defended myself. These expectations must not be satisfied, otherwise the analyst has already coacted out. After about half an hour I took leave of my patient, without scheduling another session. He left, but called me soon afterwards: "You forgot to tell me when I have to come back. I am sure my father will want to know when he comes home tonight." After that, the patient appeared regularly for his analysis.

It must be emphasized that in the case of homosexuality, psychoanalysis is not to be conducted any differently than with persons without manifest homosexual tendencies. In principle there is probably no deviation from classical technique that would further or facilitate the treatment of homosexuals. Theoretically, the ideally analyzed psychoanalyst would have no difficulties with the analysis of homosexuals. The justification for special technical directives remains almost entirely within the framework of those dangers to which the analyst is exposed by his or her own, unconscious coacting out. Even so, the following guidelines may be established:

(1) Intentions of seduction and effects of infantile sexual curiosity probably always play a role in the transference, but the responsiveness of the analyst's unconscious varies. Even though differences among individual analysts do exist, the homosexuality of an analysand seems quite generally to increase the susceptibility of the analyst's unconscious. It therefore is advisable to take particular care in the analytic situation not to reveal personal attitudes and opinions regarding homosexuality.

(2) Analysts should abandon their desire to cure the homosexual. Then they will no longer have to wait anxiously for a turn towards heterosexuality in order to feel self-confirmed.

Frequently, in the terminal phase of analysis, neurotic homosexuals, who actually are not genuine homosexuals, no longer admit the analyst as a voyeuristic witness if heterosexual strivings begin to assert themselves in practice. The analyst will then no longer want to satisfy his curiosity without having to reckon with severe setbacks.

(3) The neurotic homosexual's desires for dependence must be recognized at an early stage. They should be integrated into the interpretation work as soon as they manifest themselves as resistances to transference, since even a slight rejection by the analyst of the desire for dependence will be experienced by the patient as a severe narcissistic offense. Neurotic homosexuals cannot easily bear the frustration of their desires to be loved and accepted. They tend to form an overly strong bonding to the analyst quickly and then to repress it again. In this state, the oral aggressions, the piercing, destructive impulses appear under the guise of sado-masochistic attitudes, fantasies, memories, and associations and can no longer be pursued to the point of oral fixation because they are acted out—often manifestly—in a homosexual manner.

(4) Particularly with neurotic homosexuals who are strongly inclined to act out, and, in my experience, with women who hide their homosexuality, it is not the clinical manifestations of homosexuality that should be addressed but rather the regressive traits of narcissistic and sado-anal attitudes and characteristics. The more consistently this technique is applied and the homosexual consequences are set aside, the more systematically the analysis can progress on its course towards the enlivenment in transference of the oral regression.

(5) The demand for homosexual abstinence during analysis is comparable to a coacting out by the analyst, because any attention in that direction overestimates the patient's homosexuality and accommodates his unconscious wishes.

(6) Coacting out by the analyst endangers the analysis of homosexuals more seriously and more irreversibly than any other analysis. Modifications of classical technique such as have repeatedly been proposed—for instance, to have the homosexual sit up in a chair for a while and to interrupt the analysis without compelling reasons—are, I believe, inappropriate. The fantasies and disturbances they cause in the transference can have severe consequences. Changes produced in such a manner can no longer be assessed.

When a classical analytic situation with a neurotic homosexual has been established successfully and the patient's acting out can be systematically broken down in analysis, the question arises as to how the contents of early childhood and the meaning of the symptoms in homosexuality should be applied in the interpretational work.

It is highly probably that neurotic homosexuality cannot be reduced to a single formula. Experience shows that correct interpretations always take place without difficulties if the analytic situation has been strictly adhered to and if, first of all, the expressions of transference and resistance have been considered and interpreted in the proper sequence. Three segments from the analysis of the young man who was accompanied to the first session by his father should illustrate this.

After approximately thirty analytic hours, the patient began acting more and more exhibitionistically. He started bragging about his homosexual partners and showing off during the analysis. His complaining tone of voice was striking. I interpreted for him his lack of pleasure in his exhibition. This meant I did not accept his challenge. If I had interpreted only his showoff attitude and said, for instance, that he needed to demonstrate to me how important homosexuality was to him because, in reality, he was afraid of treatment, I would have entered into a situation of struggle with him. And if I had interpreted only the masochistic side and perhaps said, "The complaining tone of your voice shows how much you actually do suffer from being a homosexual," I would equally have accepted his unconscious challenge.

The lack of pleasure in the exhibitionist tendency (not the homosexual tendency) could be considered for interpretation, because I thus covered the phallic-narcissistic as well as the masochistic impulses and brought them into actual relation with the transference. I told him, "Your voice sounds sad and joyless even as you try so hard to show me what brings you the greatest satisfaction in life." The patient himself now emphasized the lack of pleasure in his entire life, on the one hand, and how much, on the other hand, he needed homosexuality as compensation for that lack of pleasure. I repeated that therefore it was particularly conspicuous that his voice sounded joyless and sad when he was trying to demonstrate to me how much homosexual experiences satisfied him. Now, annoyed, he turned towards me and began questioning the sense of getting treatment. The interpretation had caused a disappointment in the transference.

It is a remarkable experience to learn that neurotic homosexuals generally remain untouched by the criticism of their behavior by those around them. In making my patient aware of his showing off or his masochistic traits, one might even have used insulting tone, as his father did, without offending him. However, if one simultaneously touches both unconscious defense positions with an often seemingly harmless remark, one discovers how vulnerable these homosexuals are in their self-esteem.

Thus, the interpretation of his lack of pleasure in his exhibition did indeed result in offending my patient. He reproached me that I did not understand him. Then he demonstrated his dependency, filled with anxiety, in the relationship with his father. He felt persecuted by him. I interpreted to him that the desire to be recognized and loved by his father was hidden behind the dependency and fear. The early interpretation of his desire for dependency was important in order not to repress the positive transference, compromised by the offense that had come about. The interpretation of the wish to be loved by his father resulted in a change in transference. Now he drew libido from his homosexual friends and devalued them, and the desire for love was transferred onto the analyst, but in the form of the fearful dependency that he had previously experienced it with his father.

If it was consistent to interpret dependency and fear of persecution in the relationship with the father, thus providing the transference with strong and positive impulses, the same interpretation of dependency and fear, as they now became apparent in the relationship with the analyst, would not be suitable, for the analyst would thereby follow an unconscious intention of seduction by the patient. The interpretation of that fearful dependency would confirm the patient in his passive-masochistic attitude and make the analyst appear to be in a phallic-narcissistic position. This development will become apparent in the analysis, but it must be the result of the patient's projection, not of the analyst's interpretation. Unconsciously, the homosexual patient attempts to establish such a relationship with the analyst in order to exchange roles with him. The desire to be homosexually loved by the analyst restricts itself at this stage of the analysis entirely to the desire to experience with him the sadomasochistic game of an exchange of roles. My patient was waiting for it; moreover, he was lying in wait for the interpretation stating that he was in some type of dependency because he felt the urge to deny the interpretation with words and deeds and thus to put the analyst into the passive role. A homosexual patient might respond to such a premature interpretation, for instance, that he believes the analyst erred because the analyst himself was distressed; he might say that he had noticed the analysts's sad expression even at the beginning of the session.

My patient's intent to seduce became particularly apparent when he began more and more openly to vituperate and debase his

homosexual partners. My interpretation did not proceed according to my patient's wishes but referred rather to the undemanding
nature of his choice of friends. I said, "It is remarkable that a
young man like you cannot find better partners and friends."
Finally I was able to demonstrate to him how he debased himself
with these choices. This interpretation resulted in the fact that
the patient had to demonstrate, on his own person, how devalued
and debased he must be as a fantasized love-object of the doctor.
He took a passive-masochistic attitude towards me and his dependency became even stronger. At the same time, the curiosity to
find out whether his doctor could become a homosexual partner
grew ever more apparent.

The patient had identified with me. I now represented his
person at the phallic-narcissistic level of regression, while he
acted the role of the partner at the sado-anal level. The time had
now arrived at which infantile sexual curiosity intervened in the
transference in order to investigate the partner's seducibility. The
patient had to investigate whether his new partner, the analyst,
met the preconditions that made him appear attractive enough to
remain with him further. In accord with the patient's desires, the
analyst was to declare himself ready to exchange roles. The patient's
curiosity became increasingly direct. Finally he asked me about
my attitude towards homosexuals. I told my patient that he was
identifying me with his father, who had asked me this same
question at the beginning of the treatment. The analyst must be
prepared for such questions and decide how to confront them. In
this case, it was relatively simple to find the correct way, since the
father, on the occasion of the first meeting, had already seen to it
that the son would inevitably have to end up in his role.

Naturally, the patient was not satisfied with my answer. He
reproached me for evasiveness and accused me of cowardice. I
made use of the events of the first meeting and explained to the
patient in detail how it had been at that time. He tried to turn
things around and fought against the undeniable reality of that
first session, in which his father had taken part. Subsequent to
this phase of the analysis, which neither satisfied nor interpreted
the patient's inquisitive desires, he regressed to an oral state of
clinging. Fantasies of an oceanic merging with objects and genital
parts accompanied this regression. In my experience, the analyst
at this point should not go into pregenital tendencies, and should
also avoid interpreting the fantasies, because the entire positive
transference had receded into this regression and, confronted

with the serious failure arising from my reticence, had found temporary satisfaction in those fantasies.

My attention was directed more profitably towards the acts of revenge the patient was unconsciously planning, in order to punish me for the failure he saw in my attitude. He provoked his parents into a negative attitude towards the analysis by no longer taking care of himself and by leading an increasingly disorganized life. It did not take him long to start reporting the complaints of his parents. At the same time, he again became more cheerful and active during his analytic hours. I interpreted to him his secret intention to incite his parents against the analysis so that he could submit passively to their wish if they should demand the termination of the analysis. This prospect, I added, made him, after a long time, once again cheerful and venturesome.

At that point the provocations stopped, but the patient did not relapse into his passive-submissive attitude; however, he did take the dirtiest of men to bed with him. The analyst must not be influenced by the increased homosexual activity of his patients and attempt, say, to counteract such apparently unfavorable developments by setting down conditions or using threats, advice, and suggestions. It is more consistent and logical to address oneself to the interpretation of the unconscious strivings originating in the oedipal points of fixation. I interpreted to the patient his identification with his parents' demands and told him that he was demonstrating, with his dirty partners, what the parents thought about the analyst. Subsequently, I always interpreted only how he had identified himself with his parents and partners. This interpretational work led to a change in his behavior. Whereas until now he had actively sought his friends in order to get himself passively seduced by them, he now let himself be found passive in order to seduce his partners actively. With increasing clarity, this change in his behavior became the focal point of the observation and was interpreted in the transference as an attempt at identification with the analyst. Not until now were the dependency and fear, transferred at an earlier point from the father to the analyst, interpreted as the expression of a repressed desire to be loved by his doctor.

The change the patient demonstrated with regard to his homosexual partners was the consequence of the identification with the analyst. It was the first result of the transference neurosis, which develops with such difficulty in manifest homosexuals. I consider it a significant factor in the technique of treating homosexual patients that this process of identification in the transference is interpreted and worked through only when the process begins to manifest itself in a change of behavior in the contact with homosexual partners. Usually the patient will be unable to bear this interpretation and will respond with a regression. This will often be followed by an apparent waste of time. The analyst begins to doubt whether his procedure was correct. He tires of calmly watching the regressions demonstrated by his patient. Finally, though, the patient will work through the interpretation of his accomplishment of identifying with the analyst and will be able to adhere to his new mode of behavior without having to reject or repress the significance for the transference, which also forms part of the inherent content of his behavior. This interpretation of the identification with the analyst is so important because the repression of the oedipal desires occurred in the identification with the mother and, consequently, the identification is a constant reminder of the castration anxiety. The neurotic homosexual cannot identify without entering into a regressive cathexis, which, in his case, is supported by the interchangeable points of fixation. By means of transference, he now has to relearn how to undertake an identification free of anxiety and how to enter into it without following the ever ready cross-over mechanism between phallic-narcissistic and sado-anal cathexis. Once this process takes place in the transference, the patient will orient himself, still very unsteadily and only within the analytic relationship, according to the phallic-narcissistic mode of experience characteristic for the nonneurotic homosexual.

This was the case with my patient after it became bearable for him to have his friends find him passive and to seduce them actively, even though he was aware of the significance of his identification with me. At that point, the acting out receded into the background and a stream of memories concerning the relationship with his mother took up the analytic sessions. After that, interpretations of the transference were avoided. Connections demonstrating the patient's identification with his mother were clarified.

When the analysis with a neurotic homosexual has progressed to this extent, analysts are threatened by a very remarkable temptation. They feel quite satisfied in their analytic role and think that the time has arrived to provide the patient with interpretations that go far beyond the theme of identification with the mother. The homosexual patient will in fact do almost anything in order to get the analyst to do so. He will bring profound material in which the castration anxieties appear so clearly in their connection with the father that it becomes difficult not to interpret them.

He will also show his incestuous desires and will occasionally speak quite openly about his longing, as a child and as an adult, for sexual relationships with his mother or his sister. I believe one does not err if one regards also these reports as an unconscious intention to seduce. The renouncing of the tendency to act, which must be maintained during this phase of the analysis, refers almost entirely to the fact that the analysts restrict themselves to interpret only the identification with the primary female person in childhood.

The second phase of the analysis to be reported here began at approximately the 160th hour. Externally, the analysand was changed; although well groomed and elegantly dressed, he seemed rather clumsy in his behavior. A childlike, naive trait was unmistakable. He hung on to his analysis and fantasized that he wanted to become a very successful man, an architect like Le Corbusier, a politician like Churchill, or a rich businessman. He didn't yet know. To every frustration in his daily life he responded with a homosexual act. He took up position somewhere and waited until a partner came along. Then he seduced him. Every time he reached this point, he suffered a depression.

The phallic-narcissistic attitude was clearly recognizable. The homosexual act with which the patient responded to each frustration had now taken the place of the earlier sado-anal regression. The homosexual activity was no longer an expression of the double-tracked regressive process of adaptation. In a certain sense it became a plagiarism of itself. The depressions indicated that homosexuality no longer really suited him. He found gratification in masturbation; he phantasized that a strong heterosexual man was passionately in love with him. Reporting such fantasies, he clearly became increasingly depressed. The interpretation affected the connection between satisfaction and depression. I told him he was sad because his doctor was not the one with whom he had sexual relations.

If during the first phase of the analysis it was apparent that the interpretation of his desire to be loved by me could not be provided, it must be emphasized that at this point it became important to broach these desires candidly. After the patient had changed to the extent that he could bear a phallic-narcissistic libido position, there was no reason to hesitate in interpreting manifest homosexual desires in the transference. The analyst must be able to take into account that he might be considered the object of direct homosexual demands. If he manifests internal inhibitions here, a repression of his own homosexual impulses is present.

The interpretation was important at this point because only

thereafter would the patient be able to work through the new experience in his relationship with the analyst — the experience of feeling loved and yet forgoing sexual gratification. My patient certainly had not reached that point. He showed a reaction of disappointment in the transference and turned negativistic. I interpreted the disappointment. He became reproachful and accused me in an irrational manner. The reasons for the projection could be found in his fantasies. It turned out that his doctor had appeared in his masturbatory fantasies. During this time, the patient regressed to his homosexual activities only when the failure to act in the analysis seemed unbearable.

Exhibitionist tendencies that had been present at the beginning of the analysis gradually reemerged. However, the demonstrative behavior and the showing off were directed at women. He took a masochistic girl to the movies and made fun of her. I showed him his arrogance and told him he seemed naive because he did not know women. This caused him to experience a narcissistic offense, which resulted in a regression. He became passive-masochistic within the analysis and complained about his fate. Outside the analysis he found remarkably nice friends who were not homosexual. He conceived a plan to seduce the youngest ones among them homosexually. The patient expected that now the analyst would finally object and reveal himself as an enemy of homosexuality. However, my interpretation concerned his hidden unpleasure, which became clearly apparent in the attempts to seduce his new friends. My patient thereupon became aggressive and reproached me with jealousy. He reviled me and psychoanalysis. In rapid succession the entire family opposed the analysis.

Accompanied by a triumphant son, the enraged father appeared at the next session and said: "Everything is spoiled, the great hopes have vanished, confidence is violated, the money thrown out the window." Without providing any explanation, I rejected all these rebukes and emphasized that the analysis must be continued. It was not possible any other way. The father threatened to pay no longer for the treatment. As he was about to leave the consulting room with his son, I called to the patient to come back to his session. Reluctantly, he obeyed. Then he began to cry.

Working through this dramatic scene led to the interpretation that the enraged father had taken the place of the analyst. Since the patient had not succeeded in getting his analyst to intervene, he seduced his father to do so instead. It became clear that, in the transference, the analyst had taken on the role of the homosexual seducer. The patient found himself in the role of the person of the young friend not yet seduced. His father rushed to his aid in order to frustrate the "evil intentions" of the analyst. Thus the patient understood that he himself had a hostile attitude towards his homosexuality. The hostile attitude towards the analyst, which was connected with it, remained untouched in its significance for the transference. The further working through revealed, tentatively, that the young, not yet homosexually seduced boys were to be the girls he yearned for. However, they were no more than a displacement substitute for the analyst, who in his fantasies turned into a frightening woman, ready to destroy her victim. Thus the *mater castratrix* took on transference significance.

The third segment we want to select out of the analysis developed after approximately three hundred analytic hours. That was one year before termination of treatment. For a long time the patient reported only infrequently, and very little, about his homosexual experiences. In general, erotic interests played a much lesser role than previously; professional and family problems were more important to him. Enraged, he began to protest against the passivity of his mother, who, when the slightest demand was made upon her, responded with an illness. The decreased interest in erotic experiences was the result of the castration anxiety, which became increasingly threatening in the transference. The dammed-up instinctual impulses increased the tension that had earlier been discharged in the protest against the passivity of the mother. Fundamentally, he protested against his own passivity, which meant, in fact, his comparative sexual abstinence.

The guilt of the father with regard to the sufferings of the mother came up for discussion. The rejecting attitude of the father had worn the mother down. Then the patient became protective of the father and accused the mother. She now was guilty of the father's rejecting attitude. The exchange of roles was experienced once more, now with the prominent figures out of childhood. As soon as he became protective of his mother he experienced himself as passive, and the father as the phallic aggressor. If he took the side of his father, the mother became threatening and endangered by his own aggression. Only in these fantasies, which dealt with the question of guilt, did the phallic-narcissistic and the sado-anal wishes, in their oedipal significance, finally become part of the analysis.

When the father now praised him, he reacted with anxiety. He believed he had been lured into a dangerous trap by the analysis. He could find no reason for his worries. An ever greater confusion developed in him. In this confusion, the entire oedipal problem was traced back to the patient's oral fixation, which now became effective in the transference. He changed his attitude and eagerly sought new homosexual experiences. Without discrimination, and without satisfaction, he would go to bed with a series of men during the course of one evening. Finally, he found a repulsive, older man. In a compulsion to confess, he described all details of the homosexual act, but kept his own feelings quiet with particular stubbornness. Resisting furiously, he finally admitted that great revulsion, impotence, and shame had arisen within him. A phimosiectomy, which he had kept secret up to now, superficially motivated his fear of having too small a penis. By now he wept in almost every session; he asked me to help, he neglected himself, he stopped working, and he stated, without affect, that he wanted to kill himself. In dreams and fantasies, the experience with the old homosexual man reappeared again and again in distorted form. He found himself in the midst of a severe regression in which nothing seemed to have substance any longer.

The working over of the homosexual experience with the old man took place in the transference, in that I was able to show to him he was seeking me and his father when he submitted to that revolting partner. What he found, instead, in his projected fantasies was not a father but a horrifying castrating mother. The image of the old man disintegrated into its individual parts during the analytic work. Age meant sexual maturity. That which was revolting was motherly. He experienced the greediness in the gaze of the man as a threat of castration by the father. The entire picture concerned the threatening role of the analyst within the oral regression. The patient felt that analysis exacted an enormous demand he was unable to fulfill. This demand had as its meaning that the analyst would like to devour him. The patient offered himself, in his entire persona, as a victim. In this annihilation anxiety, he experienced castration anxiety on the oral level of experience.

The patient had made the greatest efforts to protect his homosexuality, once acting in a phallic-narcissistic manner, then again in being sado-masochistically submissive. He attempted by all possible means to reactivate the double-tracked regressive adaptation in order to defend himself against the much more deep-reaching and threatening oral regression. This attempt, however, did not succeed, because meanwhile the system of the phallic-narcissistic and sado-anal points of fixation had fallen victim to the transference neurosis. The patient found himself in a pregenital state, which is compared, not without good reason, to prepsychotic syndromes. It should be added, though, that this development occurred through the change in the meaning of the transference and thus was a result of the analysis. That was also the reason for the fact that the interpretations regarding the significance of the associations caused the regression gradually to disappear.

The contents of the patient's fantasies and experiences were worked through for many weeks thereafter, until he gradually learned to differentiate the projections from the references to reality. Thus, unperceived by the patient, the regression became less and less urgent. During the subsequent development, the analyst no longer needed to expect an increase in the transference. However, he was able to observe how, after the castration anxiety was overcome, the patient's erotic interests had to be examined and measured again and again against the transference to the analyst. With the decrease of transference tension, achieved by means of interpretational work, the necessity to compare his love objects gradually decreased.

To what extent homosexual desires, fantasies, and acts keep playing a role in the life of a patient, even after termination of the analysis, depends upon whether neurotic homosexuality is a symptom or whether the neurosis consists in the inability to accept an undisturbed homosexuality. I have not discussed this in the clinical example presented here, because it seemed important to me to focus my observation upon the neurotic disturbances that may emerge in the development towards homosexuality or in a neurosis with homosexual symptoms. If homosexuality is a symptom, then the homosexual inclination can reappear again and again under all kinds of emotional stresses. The crucial question is whether alternatives other than regression are available and could be cathected. It is the task of analysis to open up such possibilities. It cannot be the aim of an analysis to replace an obsession to follow instinctual impulses with an obsession to repress them.

When the transference of the neurotic or nonneurotic homosexual gradually grows weaker, a difficulty arises in the unconscious of the analyst. Owing to the particular form of the analysand's transference, the analyst's own countertransference often has become strong and ambivalent. In such moments, analysts may easily be seduced into demanding confirmation of their analytic work. They would like to know what the priorities are in the analysand's sexual life, but as a rule they get to hear no more about it. They then must take care not to ask questions of the analysand. If they will remember the difficulties they themselves had with the analysand's curiosity during the cure, it will become easier for them to forgo such questioning. Their psychoanalytic understanding will reimburse them for their sacrifice.

4

ON THE GENESIS OF A DISTURBED SEXUAL IDENTITY, BASED ON THE MODEL OF HOMOSEXUALITY WITH NARCISSISTIC PROBLEMS

In this section I will focus on psychoanalytic experiences which we have gained from the transference and which show us earlier states of sexual identity in repeated form, and evaluate them as to their significance for later development of the gender role and sexual behavior. When observing cases in which disturbances of sexual identity are apparent but the total persona is not so severely disturbed that we would have to speak of a psychotic development, we are faced with a number of clinical pictures. What they all might have in common is difficult to say.

My considerations are based on experiences with analyses of patients whose infantile instinctual vicissitudes resulted in a special form of neurotic homosexuality. The clinical picture of homosexuality is genetically not uniform. What finally results in a specific gender role has manifold constellations and configurations at its base. Psychoanalysis has developed a series of models and concepts allowing us to understand the various developments that give rise to a neurotic homosexual object choice.

On the basis of on my own observations, I wish to demonstrate how much evidence there is to support the fact that—in the case of certain homosexuals with narcissistic problems—a dissimilarity between instinctual development and ego development, a disproportion between the lines of development (according to the theory of Anna Freud), can result in disturbances of sexual identity. I believe that instinctual development and ego development progress at different rates during the late preoedipal phase. Whereas a

55

slowing down in the area of ego development results in a lingering in magical thinking, a relative acceleration in the area of instinctual development produces a deficit in the functions controlling sexual and aggressive strivings. This leads to an insufficient integration of the total personality. I believe that with certain neurotic homosexuals such a disharmony between the lines of development must be assumed because these patients have a noticeable tendency to experience practically everything that is connected with the sexual differentiation between the genders by way of regression, in terms of superiority versus inferiority, strength versus weakness, and omnipotence versus impotence. This tendency, characterized by clinging to magical thinking, aims to keep the form of the imagined sexual representations undetermined. In their thinking, these homosexuals frequently follow a cliché when they imagine the differences between man and woman. Their views impress us as being undifferentiated.

Within a personality that is otherwise differentiated, traits become apparent that feel like foreign bodies. In addition to other aspects, whose significance should not be underestimated, the development towards neurotic homosexuality with a narcissistic disturbance constitutes an attempt to avoid sexual differentiation and to cling to an image which anatomically is still undifferentiated and in which disparities in power play a decisive role. The unevenness between ego development and instinctual development resulted in the fact that the child discovered the anatomic differences of the sexes before a certain maturity in the development of self- and object representations had been achieved, a maturity that would have made possible a critical, realistic appraisal of that which the child had discovered.

Let me point out briefly the observations that have confirmed my perception. In the analysis of narcissistically disturbed homosexuals it is noticeable that the patient in many cases attempts to force the analyst into an intolerant attitude towards homosexual tendencies. The assumption that superficial rationalization, the hostile attitude of society, and the analysand's wish to gain the analyst's esteem are the reasons for this behavior does not suffice to explain the stubbornness of this tendency. Rather, one must assume that this is a matter of repetition in the transference that mirrors an earlier situation, in which one parent was adverse to the bonding of the child with the other parent. Such an experience can have a traumatic effect and may result in a disappointment in the parents' perfection, through which the formation of the idealized parental imago is partially suppressed. The internalization of the idealized parental imago that should follow in a later phase is thus disturbed. This constellation then leads to the preference of those object relations which permit a feeling of increasing power in self-esteem. The inclination to prefer certain object relations in this manner can also be observed in the analytic relationship and is related to the patient's difficulty in accepting the analyst's tolerance. This difficulty emerges regardless of whether the analyst is of the same sex or not, and also regardless of whether the analyst represents the role of one parent or the other in the development of the transference. This seems to me a noteworthy indication of the fact that sexual differentiation does not yet play a part in the narcissistically disturbed homosexual.

In connection with the patient's need for omnipotence, it is worth mentioning the desire of such homosexuals to provide themselves with almost all gratification by means of autoerotic activities. In this manner they aspire towards the image of self-perfection. This tendency is also characteristic of nonneurotic homosexuals, although their striving for inner and outer autonomy goes far beyond the sexual sphere. Usually, narcissistically disturbed homosexuals are noticeably easily offended when they get close to someone. This applies when they enter analysis, but often also in their encounter with their homosexual partners. However, as soon as such analysands begin, in the further course of the analysis, to transfer the unconscious, idealized parental imago onto the analyst, the narcissistic vulnerability decreases to a noticeable degree. Gradually it becomes obvious that the narcissistic equilibrium can be maintained only as long as the analyst is experienced as a sexually undifferentiated person. But as soon as the analyst is recognized as a person with sexual characteristics—or, in more general terms, as soon as anatomic-sexual aspects regarding sexual differences come to the fore—one can observe that every utterance of the analyst is accepted or rejected as though the analyst were striving towards some sexual aim with the analysand. The notions of being sexually overwhelmed, destroyed, or castrated are playing their part here. Analysands react less with fear than with a feeling of being drained of the possibilities to provide themselves with narcissistic gratification.

The phallic, sadistic, and aggressive fantasies, as well as the feelings of jealousy and rivalry, that are reported by these patients in such phases of the analysis indicate that the sexual polarity of the parents was frequently experienced as an aggressive relationship of the parents towards each other. One parent always appears as the aggressor, the other as victim, whereby the fantasized aggressor can be either the father or the mother. Increasingly one gets the clear impression that all activities of the parental figures were experienced as overwhelming and debasing sexual activities, and that the patient's comparison of these parental figures with himself was so disappointing and discouraging that a threatening sense of impotence and helplessness resulted.

In this connection it seems to me that the structuring of the object relationship towards which the homosexual is aspiring in general is of special significance in analysis. It is amazing to realize over and over again with what ease and flexibility the homosexual can take up and relinquish object cathexes. There exists a constant oscillation between object cathexis and self-cathexis, in which the processes of identification and projection play a major part and observing and comparing take on particular significance. I have experienced that this oscillating always appears when interest, even from nonneurotic homosexuals, becomes directed towards the analyst as a sexual object, whereby the patients continuously compare the sexual properties they ascribe to the analyst with the image they have of themselves, of their bodies, and of their sexual capabilities and accomplishments. At this point the neurotic homosexual usually escapes into homosexual acting out. In such phases, the often aggressive, phallically exhibiting patient experiences the waiting and tolerant analyst as passive-submissive and, in this impotence, helplessly at the mercy of the patient. If the analyst attempts to intervene, a change of role often occurs. The patient now appears passive-submissive and helpless, while ascribing phallic power to the analyst. In these phases, narcissistically disturbed homosexuals attempt to identify with the idealized analyst. If the identification is successful, the patients themselves feel phallic and powerful; they then proceed to project the threatening feelings of powerlessness onto the analyst. If the identification is not successful, the idealization is withdrawn and transferred onto a suitable—usually homosexual—partner. In the compulsion to repeat to which such patients are subjected, the idealization seems to be continuously in the service of the defense against feelings of powerlessness and narcissistic offenses. If the analyst perceives this need of the patient for idealization as defense, then the change of roles can repeat itself in quick sequences, so that a tacit battle between analyst and patient ensues. This development can lead to an unfavorable progression of the treatment. From the standpoint of the development of transference, such patients are compelled to establish over and over again, almost by way of trial, a sexual polarity in the analytic relationship. This step towards sexual differentiation frequently fails, with the result that the conflict in which these patients find themselves with their analysts revolves, in an undifferentiated manner, around disparities in power.

In reality, narcissistically disturbed homosexuals are unable to maintain the cathexis of the idealized object. In order to arrive at a more realistic structuring of the unfocused conceptual representation of their body-ego, they make use of the omnipotence-impotence role-playing as a means for testing reality in their object relations. Their efforts are useless attempts at healing; they fail because identity and object reality in the self are disturbed and because there is a lack of clarity, particularly with regard to sexual identity.

The disparities between instinctual and ego development led to the fact that the self- and object representations were still permeated with the distorted images of the parents' roles when the child discovered the differences in the sexes and recognized his own sex. In these patients, the disturbances in sexual identity constantly threaten to diminish narcissistic equilibrium and self-esteem. Psychoanalytic experience shows that in these special forms of homosexuality the disharmony between the developmental lines must be understood as a narcissistic disturbance of sexual identity.

In the psychodynamic sense, the longing for the idealized object in the transference becomes ever more recognizable as the analysis progresses. The longing for a merging with the mother, for a condition where the self is still experienced as part of the object, remains in the background. From the standpoint of technique, it is important that analysts permit this development in the transference and, particularly, that they not interpret it as defense. If analysts are overly active they become the persecutors or the seducers. In reality the patient needs the analyst as part of the self. Thus the therapist is no longer an object but a function (Kohut). One must be content to be part of the self of one's patients until they have a better control of reality at their disposal.

As patients becomes increasingly able to maintain the cathexis of the idealized object, they will also be able to develop a sexual object cathexis in the transference. Then, by means of a more adequate assessment and examination of reality, they will gradually and autonomously be able to reduce the idealization and distortion they had developed in the transference. For long stretches of the analysis, following the compulsion to repeat, they will value the differences in power in the object relationship more highly than the sexual differentiation; finally they will succeed in assimilating and internalizing the reality of the fantasies of grandeur and omnipotence that they previously projected, and in having their self-esteem continuously guided by the awareness of their own sexual identity.

My aim has been to gain insight into the psychodynamic interrelationships that exist in narcissistic disturbances of the sexual identity of certain neurotic homosexual patients. It has not been my intention to limit the discussion to this circumscribed clinical picture. Rather, I want to suggest that the concept of disharmony of progress in the developments of the instincts and the ego, as well as the technical aspects that are significant in the analysis of narcissistic disturbances, be applied also to other clinical forms of disturbances of male and female identity.

5

NONNEUROTIC DEVELOPMENT
TOWARD HOMOSEXUALITY

Sexuality, in whatever form it manifests itself, can never be a neurosis, a psychosis, a morbidity. The diseased aspects can be understood only as the expression of a disharmonic development within the overall psychic realm. The assumption that the choice of a homosexual partner constitutes a symptom, that homosexuality as such makes an individual psychically ill, is an insinuation. The experience of people of all cultures shows that homosexuality is one of the possible forms that human sexual life can adopt. It is only under specific societal conditions that homosexuality is styled an illness.

Although the most noticeable thing about homosexuality is that sexual aspect which can be no further divided or reduced by means of psychoanalysis, we can describe certain regularities in the psychic development that illuminate the obvious differences in the sexual behavior of homosexuals in comparison with others. We might call these typical stations within the psychic development where, so to speak, the switches get turned. These stations are not developmental bottlenecks where unresolvable conflicts leave fixations that will induce regressive processes in later life and lead to neurosis. The turning of switches we mean here is of a different kind. Its effect will be that disturbance factors and unfavorable influences, which on one level of psychic development could cause damage, are eliminated at one of the next stations of the development, or at least reduced to the point where no damage occurs. In contrast to the previously mentioned critical developments that lead to regressions, the turns of the switches represent progressive dispositions that cause reorientations in the developmental process. Within the psychic development from infant to adult, one may differentiate three typical stations where reorientations can take place and make the nonneurotic development towards homosexuality possible.

EVENTS IN EARLY CHILDHOOD

When the infant begins to experience itself no longer as part of the mother but as an independent being defined within itself, the inner image of its own person, the *self-representation,* is gradually formed. At the same time a need for *identity* (the achievement of knowing who one is) and a need for *autonomy* (the certainty of being able to decide and act independently) develop. Depending on the stresses the child is exposed to during the severance phase, either the need for identity or the need for autonomy can be *overcathected* and move to the foreground during the formation of the self-representation. These are measures against an endangering of further development, which leave psychic traces behind. If, for instance, an infant is asked for achievements it cannot yet attain, the need for identity will be stronger than the need for autonomy, because the excessive external demands already insist on too much independence. However, if an infant is exposed to an overwhelmingly experienced, all-controlling influence which cripples its attempts towards independence, the need for autonomy will come to the fore.

In defining the image of one's own person, the relationship with one's own body plays an important part. Self-representation is always accompanied by body representation. In the identity formation it is the increasing experience of mastery over the body, and in the development of the autonomous functions it is the discovery of pleasurable body sensations, that contribute to a well-rounded image of the self. Without exception, autoeroticism plays an important role. When the infant masturbates, it is experimenting with attaining gratification without external help, that is, usually unaided by the mother. One may also say that the autoerotic gratifications of the child are instinctual acts by which the subsequent autonomous functions of the ego are planned in advance.

The first turning of the switches—which during a subsequently developing homosexuality results in a reorientation in the psychic development—takes place during the formation of the self-representations by emphasizing the need for autonomy. In early childhood this need for autonomy is gratified by an over-cathecting of autoerotic activities. This turning of the switches results in the fact that, from now on, insufficiency symptoms in the psychic equilibrium are equalized by means of an increase in autonomy within the realm of self-esteem. This can succeed by means of an overcathecting of autoerotic activities only as long as a diffuse affective state of well-being suffices to control the regulating of the psychic equilibrium. During the course of further development, higher levels of regulation become necessary—differentiations that no longer have anything to do with sexual gratification. The autonomous functions thus no longer derive their amplification and strength from autoerotism but from quite different personality sources. In spite of that, in the development into homosexuality, the regulation of self-esteem, of the maintenance of differentiated human relationships, of the ability to love, of tender and sensuous feelings—in other words, of all activities within social life—remains primarily dependent upon the autonomous functions of the personality. Only in the sexual organization of homosexuals—being the legacy, so to speak, of the first turning of the switches—is an intimate relationship between autoerotism and the striving for autonomy durably preserved. Sexual interests direct themselves towards one's own person, and towards others insofar as they are of the same sex. Dissimilar otherness is perceived, but not much cathected. Curiosity addresses itself towards what one can experience with oneself or with others resembling oneself.

The homosexual man and the homosexual woman are personalities who arrange their sexuality in a self-image in which, above all, inner and outer autonomy is guaranteed. In contrast, heterosexuals are personalities who, in their self-image, give priority to the consciousness of identity and the sense of identity. In order to feel and to know exactly who they are, they orient themselves by the polar opposition of pairs. Also homosexuals have the need to know and feel who they are, but this is of secondary concern. Their consciousness of identity can have blurred outlines without their becoming insecure. Heterosexuals, too, cathect their inner and outer autonomy, but rarely to the extent that their identity is questioned. They can enter into dependency in a more relaxed manner, because in that respect they are much less prone to conflict than homosexuals.

EVENTS DURING THE OEDIPAL CONFLICT

Once the instinctual development in childhood has progressed to the point that aim-directed wishes for love are directed outwards—which occurs at the age of three to five—every other person except the loved one is felt to be a disturbance. This results in an oedipal conflict whose fate lastingly marks later erotic and sexual life, through experiences made with the partner and the overwhelming rival, with anxiety, and with the necessary reorientation. During the oedipal phase, the infant usually develops his love relationship with one of the two parents. The infant turns to the person who responds more strongly to his expectations. As a rule, for boys this is the mother; for girls, the father. Even if the parents were homosexual, hardly anything in this process would change, because actually the parents never directly react in a sexual, but always in an aim-inhibited, manner: they sensitively adjust to the psychic impulses of their child and try to modulate the child's erotized and aggressive demands. They behave no differently towards their child than usual when they try, as gently as possible, to confront the child with societal reality. Because of this aim-inhibited reaction, the sexuality of the parents remains mute. Only at the peak of the oedipal conflict does it become the focus of the child's interest, when, through sexual curiosity, the child discovers sexual characteristics and differences and associates these specifically with the erotic feelings directed towards the oedipal love partner. The manner in which the child makes the connection between the desexualized, socially effective sexual roles of the parental figures and their biological sexual characteristics determines the subsequent sexual organization of the adult woman and the adult man. This is the second developmental station in which a turning of the switches takes place; it clarifies once more the difference between homosexuality and heterosexuality.

During the oedipal phase, the child is confronted, not simultaneously but step by step, first with the socially effective, desexualized sexual roles of the parents, and only later on with the parents' and the child's own biological sexual characteristics. This mode of observation is unimportant in the development into heterosexuality, because sexual roles and biological sexual characteristics are identically experienced as things that belong inseparably together. Such a correspondence furthers the idea of a polarized contrast between man and woman in all aspects and strengthens the personal sexual identity, which ranks first in the structure of the self-representations of heterosexuals.

In the development into homosexuality, the child's love wishes follow the preestablished tendencies to direct the interest towards one's own person or towards others similar to oneself. The boy loves his mother, the girl loves her father, simply in the same manner they learned to love themselves autoerotically, and both experience their partners as partners similar to themselves. The alien, the other, is experienced by the boy in the interfering father figure and by the girl in the interfering mother figure. Aggressive desires of removal are directed at them, whereby the fear of succumbing to these powerful figures represents the castration anxiety of the child during the oedipal phase. Because the parents react to the oedipal love desires of their child in a manner corresponding to their socially effective roles, and because their sexuality remains mute, the autoerotic ideal is delegated to the parent of the opposite sex, while the parent of the same sex becomes the interfering third party. The result is that with the discovery and the strong cathexis of the sexual characteristics, the partner selection of the oedipal love relationship is reevaluated and revised. When the boy recognizes the feared father, and the girl recognizes the feared mother, as those who are similar to them with regard to sexual characteristics, they can suddenly be considered as autoerotic partners. Accordingly, the discovery of the sexual characteristics of the mother by the boy, and likewise of the father's sexual characteristics by the girl, results in a loss of interest in those characteristics, because they now represent the other, the alien. Through this reorientation the castration anxieties are dedramatized. This does not mean that the sexually contrasting love object will be replaced by the homosexual one. The emphasis is concentrated much more on the discovery that the parent figures embody two contradictory roles. They have a double face. As long as only one face, the face of the desexualized sexual role, is recognized, the oedipal conflict is dramatized up to the formation of severe castration anxieties. But if at this point the other face of the parents is recognized, through the discovery of the sexual characteristics, the oedipal conflict is dedramatized, since the incestual desire loses its content. The Oedipus complex of the homosexual is thus submerged. In its place, a playful dealing with potential love objects emerges whose Janus-head nature seems to provide some liberating, reconciling aspects. Homosexuals identify first of all with this double-facedness of the oedipal parental figures, and in their future love life they themselves develop the typical double face that discriminates against them in the "society of polar oppositions."

The organizational pattern of the sexual role of the homosexual is composed of the two modes of experience that are the legacy of the oedipal complex. One mode of experience expresses the oedipal reaction of the child who, for the time being, has recognized only the one face of the large parental figure. Incestual wishes, rivalry, and castration anxiety result in the dramatized conflict that pushes the child into a passive-submissive attitude. The other mode of experience expresses the oedipal reaction of the child who by now has recognized the second face of the parental figure. The erotic attraction now emanating from the parent of the same sex, which was previously experienced as dangerous, results in strengthening self-esteem, which increases the personal sexual activity by accentuating the pleasurable. The two contradicting modes of experience, that is, the tendency to present oneself as passively waiting and available for submission, and the tendency to actively seek and conquer, are tendencies usually available to both partners and are constantly exchanged in the relationship.

In the relationships of homosexuals it is customary practice that one of the partners reactivates either one or the other mode of experience of the two oedipal dispositions; this occurs even during the search, the selection, and the introductory conversation, as well as during the first tentative contacts and throughout the entire staging of the sexual relationship. The pursuer expresses this in his attitude, his feelings, and his activities and thoughts. Almost as a matter of course, his partner attunes himself to the opposite of the two available modes of experience and in every regard responds accordingly, even if the roles are suddenly exchanged. This reciprocity is for both the target of their curiosity and pleasure of discovery. If both partners feel mutually confirmed, it means that they have discovered the characteristics each finds attractive in the other, namely, the readiness to exchange alternatively the roles of passive and active, the prevailing need for guaranteed autonomy in the relationship, and open access to the overcathecting of autoerotic activities. The alternating role behavior diffuses the boundaries of one's own person and makes it possible to experience oneself in the other. Thus the original autoerotic position, once responsible for the first turning of the switches, is reactivated.

If the increase of autonomy in self-esteem during early childhood derives from masturbation, that is, by means of an undifferentiated kind of regulation, then the increase of autonomy in the adult sexual object relationship—caused by the reactivation of the autoerotic strivings—serves the attainment of a differentiated, genuine love relationship.

EVENTS DURING ADOLESCENCE AND MATURITY

If sexuality receives a powerful impetus during adolescence and is expressed in a homosexual object choice, this object choice is obviously in contradiction with the norms and moral demands of society. The following discussion addresses the "coming out" of homosexuality. The coming out represents a process of consciousness in which the homosexual recognizes himself and presents himself as such. This process reveals whether or not homosexuality is consistent with the internalized image of one's own person and with societal reality. The greatest stresses to which homosexuals are exposed originate from the society in which they live. In general, society imputes to them the sexual role of unstable androgynes, slaves to their instincts. However, homosexuals, by nature, are by no means more carnal or less stable than heterosexuals. Their sexual role is defined, even though it is different from that of heterosexuals. To define this role for themselves, to form and maintain it, is the content of the conscious process of adult homosexuals, which represents the third turning of the switches in the development to homosexuality. If this step is successful, a reorientation in the life of the homosexual takes place. It is no longer primarily a matter of whether and how to be recognized and whether one feels socially accepted or discriminated against. For homosexuals it becomes increasingly a matter of striving for the arrangement of a love life free from the socially delineated modes of behavior, even though they follow them in all other matters of daily life. They must and want to adapt in order to lead a socially satisfying life. Societal pressures, prestige, and conditions regarding power and possessions dictate evaluations which are in contradiction with their love life but which, at the same time, threaten to determine it. If they cannot escape these pressures, their alternating role play in sexual behavior becomes so impaired that their ability to love is severely restricted. The very character of the homosexual ability to love lies in the fact that the ideas of masculinity and femininity, of activity and passivity, flow into each other and that sharply delineated contrasts are thus incompatible with it.

THE THREE STATIONS

One can speak of a psychosexual development into homosexuality
only if the turning of the switches took place at the three stations
described above and if the characteristic aspects of homosexuality
have been structurally integrated into the personality. The processes
initiated by the first turning of the switches are unconscious and
are integrated with the formation of the self-representations in
early childhood. The reorientation that takes place during the
second turning of the switches, during the peak of the oedipal
phase, is supported by the conscious perception and working-out
of the subjectively experienced discrepancy between sexual roles
and sexual characteristics. These processes of consciousness dis-
sipate with the beginning of the latency period of repression.
During adolescence, under the pressure of the sexual drives, the
repressed aspects reemerge in the homosexual object selection. It
is only then that homosexuality becomes integrated by means of
the constantly effective, conscious process that characterizes the
third turning of the switches. The reorientation is the result of a
conscious coming to terms with one's homosexuality and leads to
a separation between the conditions a love life requires and the
conditions that force an adaptation to society.

6

HOMOSEXUALITY

When I published an essay on psychoanalytic technique in the treatment of homosexuals more than fifteen years ago, I began with the statement that psychoanalytic research was not happy with the problem of homosexuality. I was not able to change that circumstance with my contribution, but neither could the numerous authors do so who had previously, and have subsequently, written articles and books on the subject.

It seems to me that something fundamental went wrong in the manner the questions were posed, and so, too, in all attempts to answer them. This can be demonstrated in the very delineation of what homosexuality is supposed to be. One accepts the popular definition and follows the vernacular, which describes graphic but superficial forms of appearances.

The mistake in reasoning that happened to me and many others is based on the fact that the thesis of the polar opposition between heterosexuality and homosexuality went unquestioned and was uncritically and mutely integrated into theory as a fact. Vinnai (1977) writes justifiably: "Those who persist in verifying the obvious differences in sexual behavior of homosexuals and heterosexuals will remain stuck to the surface, which must be penetrated if the decisive structural correlations are to be made visible. That homosexuality and heterosexuality are contrasted in an "abstracts" fashion means necessarily that a false consciousness, corresponding to a specific societal condition, is being applied" (p. 18).

Although psychoanalysis as a science of the unconscious emphasizes that its statements are only relatively valid, it also attempts
again and again to wrest individual aspects of its subject matter
(the human inner life) from the overall context and characterize
them misleadingly. Quite obviously, there seems to be a great need
to differentiate between the healthy and the sick, to help the
sufferers by the realization of a personal fixing of aims — in other
words, to heal everything that appears sick. Homosexuality has
been reduced to one aspect of the psychoanalytic point of view
through which the need is satisfied to differentiate the healthy
heterosexual from the sick homosexual, to help suffering homosexuals eliminate their "sexual degeneracy," to wrest them from
their infantilism of whatever type, and thus to turn them into
heterosexual personalities. Such an idealistic attitude is then placed
upon a seeming foundation of reality: homosexuality is the result
of an irreversible disturbance of psychic development and therefore has an unfavorable prognosis.

The mistake in reasoning here has to do with that entire sort of
argumentation which corresponds to a positivistic kind of thinking.
Positivistic thinking in our society is the basis of an ideology
founded on the principle of achievement. To think psychoanalytically means to think dialectically and to apply dialectically the
scientific theories of psychoanalysis.

To understand homosexuality psychoanalytically means, first
of all, to forgo the attainment of generally valid results, which
could be put into the service of a more "effective" therapy, an
"improvement" of societal abuses, or an ameliorating tolerance
for the "other." In order to put homosexuality into its proper place
in psychoanalytic thinking, it first is necessary to recall that
psychoanalysis has never made the claim to change a person. The
most important experience one can make in one's own analysis is
the experience of limitations, the restriction to the few things that
are, in fact, changeable. Not the form of conflict itself but the way
of dealing with it can undergo change. Owing to the fact that the
unconscious becomes conscious, flexibility and elasticity can
develop in the evaluation of the internal and external demands
that everybody puts on oneself and everyone feels is put on him
from outside sources. Such a process makes possible new formulations that relate conflict tendencies to the fates of the instincts,
expand modes of observation, and make what was previously
established understandable in a different way. Homosexuality is
as much a form of sexual action as heterosexuality, masturbation,
or perversion. If one applies psychoanalysis in order to com-

prehend these various forms of sexual action, one will probably understand, at most, no more than what goes on in an individual, which of his past fates of psychic development collide with the societal demands to which the person was then and is now exposed, and how the compromise, highly specific in each individual, affects his or her realm of experience.

In psychoanalytic theory, generalizations are permissible and valuable as long as they refer to psychic processes, developmental destinies, or modes of experience found in an individual case of treatment and applicable to many or most other cases. However, if one observes the specificity of a certain sexual behavior disengaged from other personality structures, a generalization is not permissible; it would be misleading. From the mere recognition that a person is homosexual, one cannot under any circumstances deduce a generally valid conflict situation that resulted in a psychopathological symptom through repression or regression. Psychoanalysis discovered infantile sexuality as the expression of the polymorphous-perverse sexual predisposition of man. However, it cannot refer solely to this discovery in order to explain mature sexual behavior, for no linear correlation exists between infantile sexual instinctual impulses and adult sexual modes of expression and experience. The question of how a nonheterosexual development could be transmuted into a heterosexual one is actually a stupid question—it aims at the realization of a "healthy world" in miniature for the individual, and it is supposed to represent a substitution for the fact that the "healthy world" at large doesn't succeed anyway. Much more interesting is the question of a possible process that owing to an acquired flexibility, creates new formulations that permit a different comprehension of what has been previously established.

The development of sexuality is closely related to psychic development and to the societal conditions in which the child grows up. The infantile sexual instinctual impulses are not simply reflections of diffuse gratification feelings on certain psychic levels of the child's development. They are much more in the service of the development of a sense of self-worth and self-esteem. On lower levels of the regulation of self-esteem there exists a diffuse affective predominance over the cognitive components. On higher levels of regulation, a cognitive differentiation develops, which moves along with decreased affective implications and leads to the desexualized achievements of the ego (Kernberg, 1977, p. 45).

This development progresses until the infantile sexual instinctual sphere largely recedes during the latency period. Not until puberty do the demands of the sexual instinct become apparent, but, temporarily with a completely new quality of experience. The fact that parts of the infantile sexual mode of experience are reactivated still by no means indicates that mature sexuality is the same—or, in regressive form, can be the same—as the infantile sexual realm. Therefore we can exclude from the very beginning the thought that homosexuality can be reduced to an infantile, immature form of the sexual mode of experience and can be explained that way. Certainly there are formations of homosexual modes of experience that, on the basis of a neurotic development, can be so regarded, but there is nothing in this that specifically regards homosexuality. Clearly analogous conditions can also be found with heterosexuals who manifest an infantile and immature mode of sexual experience as the result of a neurotic development. In these cases one would not attempt to explain the infantilism in the psychic realm by means of the specific heterosexual object selection, but would, instead, further investigate the neurotic fixations and repressions and their causes.

Sexuality, no matter in what form it shows itself, can never be a neurosis, a psychosis, or a morbidity. Anything psychopathological can only be the expression of a disharmonic development in the overall psychic realm. Under the societal conditions in which most people live, it is practically impossible to avoid an irregularity between instinctual development and ego development. However, if a disproportion between the lines of development does exist (A. Freud, 1968, pp. 66ff. and 119), effects are to be expected that render all people more or less neurotic and influence them in their sexual life, whether they behave heterosexually, homosexually, perversely, or predominantly heterosexually, predominantly homosexually, predominantly perversely, or barely perceptibly heterosexually, barely perceptibly homosexually, or barely perceptibly perversely. To understand homosexuality psychoanalytically does not mean taking on the topic of homosexuality in order to design theoretical and practical guidelines permitting one to "treat" homosexuality, since that would mean nothing more than manipulating it.

The inherent difficulty with homosexuality is that the only thing specific about it seems to be sexual. What is sexual is not further divisible; it is a phenomenon of all that lives. This is no different from heterosexuality, only that there the difficulty is omitted, because it would never even occur to one to speak of heterosexuality if there were no homosexuals. Whether one observes heterosexuals or homosexuals psychoanalytically, it is not the sexual realm that is psychopathological, resulting in symptoms that make the individual psychically ill, but, more likely, that which hinders the sexual experience, disturbs it, or makes it impossible. The assumption that the selection of a homosexual partner already indicates a symptom, that homosexuality as such makes an individual psychically ill, is an assumption. The experience of people of all cultures shows that homosexuality can be a form of human sexual life that occurs always and everywhere and is to be taken seriously. It is only under specific societal conditions that homosexuality gets stylized into an illness. The same is true with regard to perversions. The assumption, for instance, that fetishism or transvestism as such belong to the psychopathology of human mental life is disproved by numerous customs and institutions of cultures.

Although the most noticeable aspect of homosexuality is found in the sexual aspect, which can be neither further divided nor psychoanalytically reduced, one can describe regularities in the psychological development of human beings that illuminate the obvious differences in the sexual behavior of homosexuals in comparison with others. It is a matter of certain typical stations within the psychological development where, so to speak, the switches are turned. These switch-turning events are not identical with the typical epigenetic crises occurring in the course of the libidinal development. In other words, these are not stations within the course of development where special dangers lurk, in the sense of unbridgeable conflicts, such as in the transition from the anal to the narcissistic-phallic phase or during the decline of the oedipal complex. In those critical areas, fixations usually develop that can induce regressive processes later on. The turning of switches to which I am referring here is of a different kind and results from a psychoanalytic experience: Traumatic influences, which may result in psychopathological damage, occasion the further psychical development to turn switches at one of the next stations on the way, thereby eliminating damaging influences, or at least reducing them as much as possible. This is what Hartmann (1954) meant when he wrote, "What appears to be 'pathological' in a cross-section of development, may, viewed in the longitudinal dimension of development, represent the best possible solution of a given childhood conflict" (p. 34).

In contrast to the critical developments leading to regressions, the turnings of switches I am stressing here are progressive dispositions. In that connection, reorientation occurs in the developmental events. Fixations are avoided because of the formation of compensatory structures.

If in the following I examine the typical stations more closely, it should be kept in mind that, above all, I am trying to trace the undisturbed, normal development into homosexuality. Only thereafter, or at least in consideration of these points of view, is there any sense in defining the possible neurotic, that is, inner psychic, disturbances and the psychopathological processes that may develop in homosexuals. One must not forget that most homosexuals are not so handicapped by the neurotic disturbances they may have formed in the course of their development that they would ever consult a psychological counselor or a medical psychotherapist. This applies by no means only to homosexuals, but also to all others, and those others are not only heterosexuals. At this point I should like once more to emphasize that it is misleading to focus on polar contrasts referring exclusively to sexual appearances, if we want to comprehend the psychic aspects. Neurotic disturbances that may possibly emerge are not more or less severe psychopathological occurrences simply because they appear in a person of one or another sexual practice.

Within the psychic development from infant to adult, three typical stations that make a development into homosexuality possible may be defined, so to speak, macroscopically.

The first station is within the narcissistic development and relates to events concerning the delineation of self- and object representations and the emergence of the image of the self, that is, one's own person. The second station is part of the oedipal development and concerns the coming to terms with the large figures of childhood; here, the mastering of incestual desires, of castration anxiety, of problems of rivalry, and of adaptational forces necessitated by societal conditions are in the foreground. The third station, in puberty, extends beyond adolescence into adulthood. It pertains to events concerning the "coming out" of the homosexual. This is a matter of a possible, or perhaps impossible, confrontation of homosexuality with, on the one hand, the internalized image of one's person and, on the other, with the societal reality in which the homosexual lives.

In principle, the three-stage approach in the description of the development into homosexuality is equally illuminating for men and women. It would seem that differences become more visible as one observes later phases. In particular, the discrimination against homosexuals has different effects, since it partially merges with the general discrimination against women. I have arrived at the ideas I describe here mainly through the study of male homosexuals, and I have realized that the simplifying formula — that everything would be alike in females if the conditions were reversed — is an assumption. Psychoanalytic experiences with lesbians indicate that female homosexuality requires a separate examination.

OBSERVATIONS CONCERNING EVENTS
IN THE NARCISSISTIC DEVELOPMENT

The term "narcissistic development" summarizes processes that start to form during early childhood and subsequently differentiate themselves throughout one's entire life. The image everyone has of oneself is thus developed. One speaks of the delineation of the self. This image is supposed to be nice and well-rounded in order to attain a strong and stable self-esteem, capable of coping with the reality of life and the society in which one lives. When life begins, mother and child are a single unit, each a part of the other. Yet, soon and inevitably, this dual-union is disturbed, and the world of the child is no longer complete. Something is missing. A gap, a crack, a chasm appears and causes fear, resulting in an inordinate desire to remedy the disturbance, fill the lack. Through fantasies of omnipotence and delusions of grandeur, the child attempts to recreate the completeness of his world by means of fantastically distorted images of his own person and by excluding reality. These events, which must be ascribed to an infant's specific phases of development and to quite specific experiences, are summarized within the term of the grandiose self. Under the pressure of the experience of reality and the influence of a person of reference who reacts with adequate empathy, in most cases the mother, the grandiose self is revised. This revision corresponds to an energetic potential that later on will be at work in all ambitions to attain goals of any kind (Kohut, 1971b). One may also say that the revision of the grandiose self results in a stimulus that serves the striving towards the fulfillment of ego-ideals.

Parallel to these events in the narcissistic development, events of a different kind play an equally important role. They relate to the formation of the ego-ideals. In the dualistic union with the mother, the child is content with being satisfied; he is, so to speak, in love, with satisfaction. At a later point the child falls in love with the person providing the satisfaction and idealizes the great figures of his environment. He then becomes more conscious of reality and internalizes the externally directed admiration. He now discovers things within himself that he admires. Thus, ego-ideals emerge, which, together with the ambition to realize these ideals, determine the image of one's own person. Because the delineation and further differentiation of the self depend upon these two separate processes in the narcissistic development, Kohut (1977) speaks of the bipolar structure of the self. As a rule, a well-rounded, self-contained image of one's own person does not emerge. Most people suffer a sort of shipwreck during this process, because the reformation and the internalization at one of the poles of the structure of the self did not succeed. All people, in their actions, thinking, fantasies, and in what they shape creatively, are striving to fill the gap, perfect the complacent state, create the beauty of the image of the self—in short, counterbalance everything that once failed in childhood. In every case this tendency remains unconscious, without aim. There are many ways leading to what will never be more than an approximation.

The inevitable insufficiency reflecting the early mother–child relationship represents, under the most favorable conditions, a frustration that is appropriate to the specific phase. Only if these frustrations are phase-specifically appropriate for the child's experience can the reforming and internalizing processes in the two poles of the structure, as described above, occur. Inappropriate, that is, excessive or artificially manipulated influences, estranged from experiential reality, hinder the reforming processes and inhibit and disturb the narcissistic development in a manner that may result in severe defects and pathological developments later on. However, if the narcissisitic development takes its course more or less undisturbed, self- and object representations are formed that will eventually result in conceptions about the personal self and the important persons of the societal environment. While the affective parts of these conceptions control the impulses from the instinctual realms, its cognitive parts permit the orientation in relationship with other persons in the social milieu.

Most people fail when confronted by this process because the most favorable conditions almost never present themselves. Since the mastering of this process is of vital importance and, to express it somewhat dramatically, represents a psychic chance of survival, the first disharmonies along the developmental lines of the instinctual and ego developments usually have their beginnings at this point (A. Freud, 1968).

I shall limit myself to choosing just one from the large spectrum of possibilities of how such a disharmony, responsible for the turning of the switches to homosexuality, might emerge. This turning of the switches is also decisive for the transactions that develop later on, during the oedipal phase.

A relative slowing down in the area of ego development results in a persistence in magical thinking, whereas a relative acceleration in the area of instinctual development results in a weakening of the control functions affecting sexual and aggressive strivings. As I have already mentioned, such a change in the lines of development alone does not justify the inference of something psychopathological. On the contrary, it guarantees, for the moment, an important process that was threatened because of the separation problems within the mother–child dyad (Mahler, 1969). The step-by-step delineation and separation from the mother not only affects the development of the self, but is also an occurence of significance for the development of the ego and, within that development, for the formation of a functionable defense organization. Also, during this phase, individually specific instinctual destinies take form. Within these delineation processes, a line of development concerning autoerotic activities can be observed.

Regardless of the form in which they may express themselves, autoerotic gratifications play an important part throughout the entire life of every human being. They can balance disturbances in the narcissistic homeostasis. Infantile masturbation within the narcissistic development has the important function of an experimental training, so to speak, for the detachment from the symbiotic dyad with the mother—under the predominance, however, of a diffuse affective sense of well-being. When masturbating, the infant experiments with providing himself with gratification on his own and without external help—that is, usually independent of the mother. These are a child's instinctual acts, which plan in advance the later autonomous functions of the ego (Spitz, 1962).

The turning of the switches described here, which, in the development into homosexuality, represents the precondition for everything subsequent, is characterized by the overcathexis of autoerotic activities. This overcathexis can, under certain circumstances, moderate and bridge the intolerance of frustrations resulting from separation problems. The turning of the switches results in the fact that from now on insufficiency symptoms in general, originating from a relatively disturbed narcissistic development, can be counterbalanced by an overcathexis of autoerotic activities. The instinctual gratification itself is subject to a functional change, because the autoerotic activity is used to control the regulation of self-esteem. As long as a diffuse sense of well-being suffices to control this regulation, gratification and regulation are identical. That is possible only on a low level of development. During the further course of psychic development, that is, after the turning of the switches described above, higher levels of regulation are required where cognitive differentiations are predominant and affective parts of the instinctual impulses are transformed into the desexualized achievements of the ego. The functional change to which the autoerotic activities are subjected indicates that cathexis modalities, once discovered and creatively differentiated, no longer primarily serve instinctual gratification; rather, they are put to use in maintaining desexualized object relationships, aim-inhibited, tender feelings, ideal-formations, and ambitions within the social framework in which life unfolds. The self-esteem of homosexuals, their sense of identity, and also the role they play as man or as woman in society, that is, their sexual role, depend in a particular way upon the maintenance of all those ego functions and instinctual gratifications they have formed, with the help of the functional change of autoeroticism, in the total development of their personality. Autoeroticism, as phenomenon or as tendency, is not characteristic for homosexuality. With homosexuals it becomes important for certain modes of experience and behavior only because its significance is excessive later on, first during the oedipal phase and then in coming to terms with society.

Through its functional change in the narcissistic realm, autoerotism is given its primary function—the task to maintain a homeostasis. On higher levels of regulation, intrasystemic structures emerge to take over this function. If these structures are observed independently of the function's sources that define them, the following can be said.

If inanimate, unformed, and nondifferentiated objects are the focus of these structures, a perversion will arise. If an animate, highly differentiated object takes form and becomes the focal point, a mature love relationship develops.

If this animate, highly differentiated object taking form is the representative of one's own person—because the corresponding structures were formed from the functional change of autoerotism—a homosexual love relationship develops.

If this animate, highly differentiated object taking form is the representative of another person, differing from one's own person by sexual characteristics, a heterosexual relationship will emerge.

Perversion and heterosexuality are not being discussed here.

Therefore I shall not go into the sources from which those intrasystemic structures originate which take over the regulatory functions when a narcissistic disharmony threatens to appear. However, in all cases the regulation will have the function of bridging the inner contradiction between illusion and reality that continuously questions the adaptation of reality and the ability to maintain the ego structures. In other words, it is a matter of adapting the reality experiences of daily life to the unconscious ideas of the primary-process interpretation of this reality. The question is: how can the regulatory, intrasystemic structures that have emerged from the functional change of autoerotism cancel out this contradiction? How is it possible to effect agreement between illusion and reality in this way? Two tendencies may be described that at the same time indicate also the dangers of a possible neurotic development.

(1) The autoerotic experience of providing oneself with gratification autonomously and independently is quantitatively increased. A sense of special internal and external autonomy develops in the perception of the self. This tributary to the self-esteem has a stabilizing effect in the differentiation of the ego functions during the various phases of libidinal development; this effect is at work, on the one hand, in the achievements in mastering bodily functions (particularly during the anal phase) and, on the other, in the cognitive realm. Occasionally a physical and intellectual prematurity may occur. The sense of special internal and external autonomy is always maintained by means of instinctual acts whenever reality experiences place it in question. Hereby, the tendency to magic thinking becomes effective in that the increased instinctuality is interpreted in the self-perception as an increase in autonomy. This means nothing more or less than that those people who indicate a successful development into homosexuality are able to experience a self-affirmation in sexuality, like anyone else. Under the prevailing societal conditions, this self-affirmation is granted to heterosexual relationships only and, in particular, to institutionalized marriage and the ensuing nuclear family. This is connected with the superego contents that are part of the heritage of the oedipal complex. Standing by in the superego are the moral beginnings that, by means of conflicts of conscience, limit the numerous possibilities of an affirmation of a beneficent self-esteem to those which are in agreement with the prevailing morals of society.

Since the self-perception of one's own autonomy is specifically based on an overcathexis of autoerotism, interests are furthered in the homosexual that are directed at his own person, or to others insofar as they are of the same sex. The common denominator of all of them is that they overestimate their own autonomy. What is alien is perceived, but little cathected. Curiosity is directed at what can be experienced with oneself or with others resembling oneself. The dangers inherent in these tendencies are psychopathological developments stemming from the inclination to interpret relationships with others in terms of superiority versus inferiority, strength versus weakness, omnipotence versus impotence; to seek an increase of power everywhere in order to strengthen self-esteem; and, in general, to fall victim to undifferentiated stereotypical thinking, particularly with regard to differences between man and woman. The appearance of such disturbances indicates that a syntonic development into homosexuality has gone wrong.

(2) The homosexual cathects his partner, by way of trial, with libido, just as he cathects with libido, also by way of trial, the masturbatory fantasy during autoerotic activity. Because the fantasy is replaced by a partner who is real, a sexual relationship emerges that can no longer be equated with masturbation. Out of this, a love relationship may develop, which is not possible with masturbation. In this context, I must emphasize that mutual masturbation cannot be equated either with homosexuality or with heterosexuality. To masturbate together, regardless of the sex of the partner, is a sexual activity that, whether during adolescence or later, has the character of an experiment, a preparation for a sexual relationship—or, for neurotic reasons, remains fixed in its masturbatory form.

With regard to the homosexual relationship, one must emphasize not so much the trial character of the libidinal cathexis—for that plays a part in all love relationships—as, rather, the great significance assumed by this trial cathexis of the partner. This libidinal cathexis is taken over by the partner in the form of an identification or used as a fusion in order to charge the self-representations (Greenacre, 1955). This mode of cathexis is now quantitatively and qualitatively dramatized by sexuality. Quantitatively, in that the modality of cathexis begins to oscillate between self and object and is increased with sexual excitation. At the moment of orgasm a qualitative transformation takes place, since, entirely contrary to masturbation (where the leading fantasy vanishes at the point of orgasm), the unification with the real, living partner is no longer experienced as an illusionary but, rather, a real, splendid confirmation of the coherence of the personal self, as the greatest possible pleasure. Self and object fuse into one and the same, a process that is possible only if the partners are of the same sex.

In a heterosexual relationship, orgasm also leads to a fusion between self and object, but the procedure is different. The greatest possible pleasure is based on the splendid affirmation of the ability to unite with the alien, the other, which one always seeks for the completion of the personal self. If the libidinal cathexis of the alien, the other, were taken over in the form of identification in order to charge the self-representations, the leading object would lose the cathexis at the same moment the self should be cathected with it. The consequence would be an inner emptiness, and the contradiction between fantasy and reality would cause a confusion that would destroy the entire love relationship.

Among homosexuals who seek medical or psychological counsel because they despair over their homosexuality, one very frequently finds persons suffering in their love life from a neurotic object choice that goes awry. They usually differ from heterosexuals who suffer from object-choice problems only in that these homosexuals try to explain their conflicts on the grounds of their homosexuality and that they identify themselves with the societal hostility directed against them. In order to deal with the failed object choice by means of depth psychology, it is often necessary in counseling to begin by making the homosexual aware of those conditions. A neurotic homosexual object choice exists if disconcerting traits in the partner appear attractive in comparison with the image of one's own person. Under such conditions, the libidinal cathexis cannot be taken over in the form of an identification or used as a fusion by the partner in order to solidify the narcissistic homeostasis. The circumstance that the partners are of the same sex no longer suffices to overcome what appears alien in those feelings. Under these conditions, a sexual relationship cannot provide any affirmation of the coherence of the self and, along with it, a pleasurable gratification. These homosexuals, instead, suffer a severe disturbance in their self-esteem and feel an agonizing inner emptiness. Forms of neurotic object choice in homosexuals can usually be traced back to an unmastered oedipal situation. I have already indicated that it is by no means true that all homosexuals have unmastered oedipal problems simply because they are homosexuals. This widespread assumption, which is also represented in psychoanalytic theory, constitutes a prejudice that, in the manner of blinders, curtails the observation, understanding, and evaluation of homosexuality.

OBSERVATIONS CONCERNING EVENTS
DURING THE OEDIPAL PHASE

Psychoanalysis defines the oedipal conflict as a generally occurring conflict situation that emerges when, at a time of advanced instinctual development, purposeful love desires turn outwards. Every person other than the loved one is then sensed as a disturbance. At the apex of the early infantile sexual development, the libidinal desires and aggressive strivings are attached to adults. The most important point of view by far in the oedipal conflict is the object relationship. As a rule, a first love relationship is achieved during the phallic phase of instinctual development. Psychoanalysis calls this striving the incest wish. The aggressive impulses are directed towards the interfering third party. That party must be removed. The affiliated impulses here are summarized as death wishes. The anxiety of succumbing to someone stronger, which occurs in the oedipal conflict, is just as commonplace as the fact that the adult is stronger than a child. For the whole time of its duration—and that may be a person's entire life—this anxiety cannot disavow its origin in the phallic phase. Psychoanalysis calls this castration anxiety. Under our societal conditions, the conflict arising between narcissistic interests and libidinal object cathexis usually ends in the inevitable result that the incestual wish is abandoned and a simultaneously identification with the parent of the same sex, that is, with the refusing primary person, ensues, thus guaranteeing protection from the consequences of the person's own aggressive impulses.

The first conflictual coming to terms with society takes place during the oedipal phase; it is represented by the great figures of childhood. These stand for ideology, the institutions, and economic constraints that the respective prevailing conditions bring to bear upon the individual. Since the processes in the oedipal phase are affective processes, occurring in object relationships, the parents' unconscious introjections are much more significant than their personal convictions and attitudes regarding ideology, institutions, and economic conditions. They can stand in contradiction to the governing societal structure without any essential change in the role of the parents. The fate of the oedipal resolution is the fate of the human being in society. The traditional observation of psychoanalysis is usually restricted to what results from instinctual events and from object relationships: incest wish, rivalry, castration anxiety, and the establishment of the superego. These aspects are of great significance for inner psychic development. However, they contain only indirectly, and in veiled form, the societal compulsions effective from the outside. That is one of the reasons psychoanalysis has erroneously described homosexuality as psychopathology.

Since the preoedipal phases of libidinal development and, in particular, the rounding out of the narcissistic coherence are permeated with the implications resulting in the turning of the switches previously described, the oedipal conflicts and castration anxieties appear to be influenced by the primary-process interpretation and cannot be defined as oedipal according to traditional psychoanalytic interpretation. From the viewpoint of traditional metapsychology, a development into homosexuality can therefore only be understood as a miscarriage in the oedipal conflict that leads to a regressive adaptation, a defect in the development—a thesis I myself still supported as late as 1962. In order to understand where the error lies, one must investigate what a realistic oedipal-conflict constellation means and how it is influenced by the socially and culturally delineated milieu of society.

During the oedipal phase, the child is peremptorily confronted by the society in which it lives. Usually the parents represent the societal scene. The child's previous experiences and observations take on a new emotional meaning during this phase. At the same time, experiences with the parents' modes of behavior are brought into context with their biological sexual characteristics. The parents' modes of behavior and experience are to be understood as characteristics of their sexual roles insofar as they coincide with society's expectations of what a man and father, a woman and mother ought to be. The parents' sexual roles are so much the sharper in their contours as the image they form of themselves as man and woman confirms societal expectations. However, the biological sexual characteristics differentiating man from woman do not necessarily have to coincide with the sexual roles that persons develop.

There are people, transvestites, who are able to put up with the discrepancy between the role they develop and the sexual characteristics they have. Others, transsexuals, are not able to come to grips with this discrepancy and try everything to force an agreement between their sex and their sexual role. The fact that a sexual role is not inevitably identical with the biological sexual characteristics has not yet been sufficiently acknowledged by psychoanalytic theory. This fact is particularly important for the procedures in the oedipal phase, because the child is not confronted with all of the parents' sexual aspects all at once but, rather, step by step; first, by the sexual roles of the parents, and later on, by their and the child's own sexual characteristics.

Kohut (1977, p. 227–239) writes that classic psychoanalytic theory regards the positive aspects of this period of psychosexual development as the result of the oedipal experience and not as a primary, self-contained aspect of the experience itself. He emphasizes that this primary, positive experience is based on the experience of the child's growing capacity to integrate libidinal and aggressive strivings. In this connection, integration means the forming of psychic structures that modulate the demands of the instincts. According to Kohut, this increasing capacity can develop in the child only if the parental figures respond with aim-inhibited reactions to the child's libidinal wishes as well as to its rivalrous aggression in the oedipal phase. If the oedipal manifestations are responded to by means of directly sexualized modes of reactions, or by means of counteraggressions by the parental figures, the maturing of the psychic apparatus will be prevented in a damaging way. As a rule, parents restrict themselves to aim-inhibited reactions towards their oedipal child. This means that they identify themselves with their child. They are sensitive to the psychical impulses of the child and modulate the child's libidinal and aggressive demands.

The parents influence their oedipal child in a manner corresponding to their child-rearing ideology. This ideology contains the societally effective properties of the mother as woman and the father as man. The sexuality of the parents remains silent because of the predominance of aim-inhibited reactions. It does not become the focus of the oedipal conflict until the apex of the phallic phase, when the child, driven by sexual curiosity, intensely cathects the sexual characteristics and differences with libido in a new way. The new experience emerging with this particular cathexis of the biological characteristics is brought into specific, never accidental context with the other experience, which developed from the socially effective characteristics of the parents' sexual roles. The turning of the switches, which was necessary during the early preoedipal development in order to effect compensatory structures that can moderate the disturbances in the oedipal equilibrium, is responsible for the specific connection between the two oedipal experiences.

The way in which this connection develops determines the later sexual organization of the adult male and adult female. The difference between homosexuals and heterosexuals is formed at this turning point in libidinal development. Yet, the actual difference in the love life of homosexuals and heterosexuals is found in an overcathexis of certain perceptions in the self-esteem, specific for both but oriented differently, which compensates for a narcissistic vulnerability.

It is gradually becoming apparent that heterosexuals also need a particular turning of the switches in order to round out their narcissistic coherence. But it begins at a different place. With them, a relative slowing down in the realm of instinctual development, accompanied by a relatively accelerated ego development, results in a strengthening of the functions controlling aggressive and libidinal strivings. A tendency develops to permit instinctual impulses especially at a time when the image of one's own person is sharply demarcated from the objects. This results in the fact that in later sexual object relationships one's own sexual role is experienced as being in agreement with one's biological sexual characteristics, and that these are in polar opposition to the sexual role and the biological sexual characteristics of the partner. This in turn strengthens the self-esteem and, with it, the sexual identity, which belongs to the bodily self and therefore to the narcissistic sector of the personality. Just as the overcathexis of autoerotism is no longer primarily an instinctual gratification with homosexuals, but, rather, serves the maintenance of the narcissistic homeostasis, so, too, does the overestimation of polar contrasts in the sexual roles no longer serve the instinctual gratification in heterosexuals, but, rather, strengthens the sexual identity in the self-esteem.

If the compensatory structures are centered upon an overcathexis of the bodily self—that is, the self-perception of one's own body image—then, at the apex of the oedipal conflict, the parents' socially effective characteristics—that is, their sexual roles—and their biological sexual characteristics are experienced as something belonging inseparably together. Such a congruence furthers the idea of a polar contrast between male and female in all aspects that differentiate them from each other. This idea serves the strengthening of the personal sexual identity. On the basis of this precondition, a heterosexual love relationship will emerge at a later point.

If the compensatory structures are centered upon an overcathexis of the internal and external autonomy, the socially effective properties of the parents—their sexual roles—will be experienced, at the apex of the oedipal conflict, as something which cannot be brought into congruence with their sexual characteristics. Such a separation of one set of characteristics from the other indicates that in the oedipal and all other later sexual object relationships the autoerotic position will be maintained, though in its new, object-related, formulation; this will later make it possible for sexual relationships to develop relatively independently from the societally delineated and recognized characteristics of the partners in a love relationship. On the basis of these preconditions, a homosexual love relationship will emerge.

If that happens, a turning of the switches has taken place at the second, oedipal stage of development, by means of which the step is made from an infantile to an adult mode of experience. Also in the homosexual this step implicates a massive identification, which classical theory describes as an identification with the frustrating principal figure. With the decline of the oedipal complex, this identification becomes a continuously effective structure, an introjection, partaking essentially in the establishment of the superego. In a successful development into homosexuality, it is significant that the punishing tendencies, directed by the superego against the incestuous object choice, move entirely into the background, owing to changes appearing in the ego. This happens because the new characteristics belonging to one's own person, which were acquired by means of internalizing the traits of the principal frustrating figure, are congruent with the characteristics of the principal oedipal figure of the same sex. In accordance with the dominating autoerotic position, this congruence leads to the fact that the libidinal cathexis changes polarity with regard to the object that resembles one's person. These conditions indicate that at the decline of the Oedipus complex the incestuous wish loses its sexual content. In the heterosexual, by comparison, the sexual content remains bound to the incestuous wish; therefore, the heterosexual's ego responds more perceptibly to the incest taboo in the superego than does the ego of the homosexual, which remains indifferent in confrontation with the incestuous wish and the incest taboo.

Until now, classical sexual theories have always assumed, without reflection, that the sexual role of an individual is biologically predetermined. That was only intended to cover up the demand that this role correspond to the firmly established, socially effective implications. In this connection, in fact, significant achievement of object constancy for sexual life was interpreted as if the capability of entering into and maintaining genuine object relationships were bound to the choice of a heterosexual partner. It was also postulated that autoerotism, in whatever form it was manifest, was an infantile sexual activity that hindered the development of solid and differentiated object relationships. From the psychological standpoint, these thought models do not attract attention in their utalitarian one-sidedness, since it is acceptable to understand psychological developments as healthy and normal as long as they do not contradict societal demands. In the psycho-sexual development into homosexuality, this model is doomed to fail, because the essential aspect of the procedure of the oedipal phase consists in the circumstance that the sexual roles of the principal oedipal figures are not identical with their biological sexual characteristics.

It is a presumption, rooted in a widespread ideology, to deny object constancy to homosexuals. Object constancy, a term from ego psychology, accurately describes one of the most important achievements of a healthy ego that has managed an enduring, stable separation and delineation of the self-representation from the object representations. If one may ascribe to an ego the capability to enter into solid object relationships, and to maintain them even when a postponement of instinctual gratification is required or when aim-inhibited gratifications alien to the instincts are striven for, then homosexuals do not differ from "others," particularly not from heterosexuals. They are, however, like everyone else, exposed to severe neurotic developments that may result in profound disturbances of the ego functions and therefore of the object constancy as well. The majority of healthy homosexuals hold on to their desexualized object relationships, their aim-inhibited tender feelings, ideal-formations and ambitions, and they can, like heterosexuals and perverts, lead an unobtrusive life and, thanks to object constancy, carry out socially valuable performances in all fields.

The autoerotic position, which plays such a large role in the love relationship between healthy homosexuals, cannot be reduced to self-concerned masturbatory activity. The fact is, rather, that the instinctual fate of autoerotism, which is closely related to the autonomous functions, represents the organizational pattern of the homosexual love relationship. Homosexuals depend on loving partners just as much as heterosexuals do, and they are certainly not content with masturbation, even though they may, as may heterosexuals, always revert to autoerotic gratification.

Since it is generally known that some societies in antiquity integrated homosexuality quite differently, I should like to demonstrate with a quotation from Freud that early psychoanalysis had already reckoned that there are no definitive recipes for a "healthy, correct sexuality," and that such a categorization could never be more than the expression of an ideological obsession conditioned by society. As Freud (1905) says, "The most striking distinction between the erotic life of antiquity and our own no doubt lies in the fact that the ancients laid the stress upon the instinct itself, whereas we emphasize its object. The ancients glorified the instinct and were prepared on its account to honor even an inferior object; while we despise the instinctual activity in itself, and find excuses for it only in the merits of the object" (p. 149h).

The assumption that homosexuals emphasize the instinct itself and heterosexuals the object does not, however, permit the conclusion that an uncontrolled instinctuality of the former should be contrasted to a renunciation of the instincts or an instinctual frustration of the latter. Only if one starts from the premise that social and economic power structures require a societally effective morality in order to force sexuality into predelineated tracks that follow society's interests, does it become apparent why, on the one hand, one may speak of an inferior object and, on the other, of contempt for instinctual activity. Both are value judgments, carried over into sexuality.

Society's prevalent morality, with its coercions, intervenes in the love life of homosexuals and heterosexuals alike by further burdening the overcathexes of certain patterns of experience, which exist in both groups, with additional, societally conditioned and motivated distortions. Because it is the propertied class in the prevailing society that generally maintains power by a high conventionalization of polar contrasts, this society, as a matter of course, it would seem, introduces an ideology of possession based on patriarchal standards of value into the love life of its members. In the final analysis this represents an overrating of the polar contrast of the sexual roles in the sense that masculinity is now equated with the claim to possessions and an increase in power; and feminity, with subjugation and a loss of power. Thus distorted, heterosexuality, which alone is regarded as normal by this society, no longer serves the needs of people, but rather the interests of the prevailing societal conditions.

From this point of view, our society actually puts less stress on the object than on the demand that the biological sexual characteristics be identical with certain socially effective characteristics, that is, the sexual roles. This may be contrasted with another societal morality, which, while perhaps not accentuating the instinct itself that much, nevertheless permits the relationship between the bearer of the gender and certain predelineated sexual roles to be optional and relaxed. This means that people may experience their gender and their sexual role in society as being identical, but that it need not necessarily be so. This also makes it clear that the two moral demands no longer differ from each other in that heterosexuality is the concern of one demand and homosexuality that of the other, but, rather, in that one is repressive and hostile towards the instincts, whereas the other includes heterosexuality as well as homosexuality, depending on the people's needs. If one observes what is considered a realistic conflictual constellation of the oedipal situation, while keeping in mind these structural preconditions of society, then the image becomes distorted by the ideology of possessions and power. This realistic aspect is, in its own way, equally permeated by unconscious interpretations as is that other realistic aspect which I must now use as my point of departure in further pursuing the oedipal dispute in connection with the development into homosexuality.

The child enters the oedipal phase with the self-perception of his or her own overestimated autonomy. The aim-directed love wishes, directed outward, follow the developed tendencies to direct interest towards one's own person, or to others who look exactly like the oneself. The incestuous wish that evolves leads to an intensive object relationship, usually an object relationship with the opposite sex, because of the role behavior of the parents (a role behavior dictated by society). This, however, is interpreted according to the available interests, that is, as though the beloved partner resembled oneself in every respect. The other parent, who, again in accord with the roles determined by society, is usually of the same sex, is experienced as a disturbing factor. This parent represents that which is alien. The aggressive strivings during the oedipal phase are directed at that parent. The alien must be eliminated, whereby the illusionary interpretation again results in the fact that precisely that parent who is of the same sex, and looks similar, is identical with the alien. Aggressive elimination wishes cause a rivalry conflict that creates the fear of losing out to a more powerful person.

The homosexual man loves his object quite simply in the same manner as he learned to love himself and, during the oedipal phase, loved his mother. He certainly does not deny his mother's lack of a penis in direct comparison with his own person, but instead experiences his mother quite evidently as a partner who resembles him and is of the same sex. Where there is love, the lack of a penis has no importance whatsoever. Also the homosexual woman simply loves her object in the same manner she learned to love herself, by excessively elevating the significance of her successful autoerotic activities. This achievement, acquired by the little girl with much more difficulty than by the little boy, fulfills her with a proud feeling of self-esteem, which in traditional interpretations is reinterpreted (in a manner I find suspicious) as penis envy or the wish to be a boy. This interpretation smacks of a socially conditioned degradation of women. During the oedipal phase, the little girl usually chooses the father as love object and in an illusionary manner interprets that he certainly looks exactly like her and resembles her in every way. In her feeling of love, a penis is completely beside the question for this lesbian girl. During the oedipal phase, the self-perception of the overestimated autonomy is fully enhanced in the love choice. The alien, the strange, is recognized in the interfering mother figure. Aggressive wishes of elimination are directed at the mother, and the fear of succumbing to her is the castration anxiety of the oedipal girl.

In a development into homosexuality, the incestuous object relationship is characterized not by the wish to "possess" the love object, but rather by the wish to have the sexual autonomy confirmed by the love object to which the autoerotic ideal has been delegated. The aggressions of rivalry, directed at the interfering third party, are aggressions that develop when and if this need for autonomy is questioned. The castration anxieties are the fears of the threatening powerlessness, which is feared as a loss of autonomy. Since the parents' aim-inhibited reactions towards their children are permeated by autoerotic impulses, but subjugated to the heterosexual partner choice, the child's autoerotic ideal is delegated to the parent of the opposite sex, while the parent of the same sex becomes the interfering third party. These conditions make it clear that the sexual curiosity that cathects the real sexual characteristics anew at the apex of the phallic phase is of decisive significance in any development into homosexuality. The new valuation of the sexual characteristics dedramatizes the castration anxieties. When the little girl recognizes the feared mother as the one who resembles her, she suddenly becomes a possible autoerotic partner. Accordingly, the discovery of the father's sexual characteristics results in a decrease in libidinal interest in him, because he now represents the foreign, the other. When the little boy recognizes the feared father as the one who resembles him, he suddenly becomes a possible autoerotic partner. Accordingly, the discovery of the mother's sexual characteristics results in a decrease in libidinal interest in her, because she now represents the foreign, the other.

It seems important to me to emphasize once more in this

connection that it is not the sexual role of the love object that should be considered significant in the development of these relationships. It is not a matter of exchanging the love object of the opposite sex with a homosexual object at the apex of the phallic phase. Such a point of view would again, misleadingly, push the polar contrast of the sexual roles into the foreground. What should be stressed is the discovery that the parents embody two contradicting roles. They have a double face, the head of Janus. As long as only one face of the parent's Janus head is visible, the oedipal conflict is dramatized, as classic theory aptly describes it. Severe castration anxieties, resulting from the rivalry conflict, are developed. The dedramatization of the oedipal conflict begins when the second face is recognized through the discovery of the parental figures' sexual characteristics, because the incest wish loses its sexual content. With homosexuals, the oedipal complex begins to subside at this point. It is replaced by a playful association with objects whose Janus face has liberating, conciliatory aspects. The homosexual recognizes, consciously or unconsciously, that all people who may be considered as love objects or as punishing authorities have a double face. Homosexuals identify primarily with this double-facedness and they themselves, in their future love life, develop the typical double face that will disqualify them in the company of "polar contrasts."

The society we live in rejects these traits of double-facedness. The randomly alternating exchange of roles does not fit the organizational and economic interests of a society that forges an unassailable unit out of gender identity and the socially effective characteristics of thinking and behavior that are part of the sexual roles. However, rejection and hostility are not consciously directed at these traits of the homosexual; rather, they are projected onto their sexual behavior. The cause of this projection is a social hostility towards an altogether natural trait in man, which may perhaps be observed most clearly in children and in peoples of some other cultures. It is the need to search for an inner "second face" during heightened erotic and aggressive tensions in interhuman relationships that might dedramatize the threatening conflict, turn the deadly serious dispute into harmless play. It is becoming clear that the hostility towards these natural human tendencies has absolutely nothing to do with the hostility towards homosexual activities. The constraints imposed by society, which so decisively determine social conditions, are far more responsible for the fact that a playful attitude towards sexuality and aggression has been made impossible. It is these conditions that cause the search for objects to be projected. Homosexuality is a downright ideal object for such projections. Therefore one may also say that each society will create the homosexuals it needs.

Homosexuals are subject to exactly the same sociological constraints as everyone else. They are no more playful or relaxed in their dealings with the world around them or in the coming to grips with their conflicts than are other people. The playful aspect of homosexuality is, rather, an inner-psychic disposition to take up, drop, and exchange—alternatingly and free of conflict—contradictory, sharply defined modes of experience and to establish in this manner contact with each individual partner. This inner-psychic disposition is the condition that must be fulfilled in order to enable homosexuals to be sexually active and attain sexual satisfaction. It is the organizational pattern of their sexual role.

This organizational pattern is composed of the two contradictory, sharply defined modes of experience that are the heritage of the oedipal complex. One mode of experience expresses the reaction of the oedipal child that has recognized only one face of the large parental figures: incest wish, rivalry, death wish, and castration anxiety lead to the dramatized conflict. The castration anxiety, because of the tendency to identify with the love object, pushes towards a negative oedipal result. This kind of experience is anal-sadistic and corresponds to a passive tendency in the homosexual attitude. The other mode of experience expresses the reaction of the oedipal child when it recognizes the second face of the large parental figures. Since the cathexis of the love object takes place according to the model of the autoerotic position, the discovery of the sexual characteristics of the same sex leads to an erotic attraction to the corresponding parental figure, experienced as a narcissistic feeling of omnipotence that demonstrates exhibitionistically the pleasure in one's own body, one's own activities, and in the discovery of one's surroundings. This second mode of experience is phallic and corresponds to the active tendency in the homosexual attitude.

In practice, the anal-sadistic attitude corresponds to a tendency in the one partner to make himself passively available to the other. The modes of behavior characterizing this attitude are traits that every homosexual knows in himself. He waits until a partner approaches, involves himself only tentatively, and turns away but reacts in such a way that he feels pursued, persecuted. In this illusory persecution lie the preconditions for experiencing oneself as passively overwhelmed when and if a relationship finally comes about.

In comparison, the phallic-narcissistic attitude corresponds to the tendency to seek and conquer homosexual partners actively. The modes of behavior characterizing this attitude are also traits every homosexual knows within himself. He goes out searching and directs his attention towards partners who are taking a wait-and-see attitude. He then approaches them, showing at first no particular interest, sometimes even a certain amount of disdain, so that the other will turn away and the game of pursuit, of persecution, can begin. If it finally reaches the point where the two get involved, the one taking the phallic-narcissistic attitude experiences a feeling of triumph in having conquered the love object.

The two contradictory modes of experience are tendencies that are normally always available in both partners and can be exchanged vicariously. If one of the modes of experience is rigid and fixed, then a neurotic development is at work in homosexuality.

In homosexual practice, it is customary for one partner, to reactivate either one or the other mode of experience of the oedipal disposition as early as during his search, his selection, and the initiating conversation, as well as during the first tentative contacts and the staging of the sexual relationship. He expresses that mode of experience in his attitude, feelings, activities, and thoughts. In matter-of-course fashion, the partner adjusts to the opposite of the two available modes of experience and responds accordingly in every respect. In both partners, the curiosity and pleasure of discovery are directed at this interaction. If they feel mutually confirmed, this corresponds to the discovery of the sexual characteristics of the other, which are the same as one's own. The resulting sexual excitation leads to the fact that the attitudes of one towards the other are exchanged alternatingly. This has an oscillating effect, which eventually results in orgasm and is responsible for the pleasurable confirmation of the coherence in the self. As in every healthy sexual activity, the pleasurable confirmation of the self-esteem is connected with the orgasmic experience. Both together bring about the greatest possible gratification in human experience.

The neurotic disturbances that may occur in the development into homosexuality are not identical with homosexuality as such, as has been erroneously assumed for decades by the traditional conception in psychoanalysis. The confusion of ideas regarding these conditions developed out of an overrating of polar contrasts in the evaluation of sexuality. Because homosexuality was, without further reflection, equated with psychopathology, a series of perceptions have arisen in the theory that are correct only insofar as they do understand the neurotic disturbances that may emerge during the development into homosexuality. The phenomenon of homosexuality becomes distorted by the generalization of these attitudes. But when the theoretical preconditions for an objective comprehension are distorted, the psychotherapeutic measures and psychoanalytic concepts of technique based upon such a misunderstanding are fraught with danger.

In psychoanalytic theory, the homosexual object choice is defined as inversion, which means that the homosexual man identifies with his mother in order to escape castration anxiety. The same is said of the homosexual woman, except that here one is supposed to proceed from the fact that the entire development is founded upon the fantasy of the woman to be a man. Thus the phenomenon of homosexuality is stylized into a matter of dependency-psychopathology, which, in its mildest case, is said to be recognized in an incestuous fixation upon the oedipal love object, and in severe cases are said to lead to a pathological symbiotic fusion approaching psychosis. For instance, the traditional conception is derived from the assumption that the incest wish succumbs to repression, with a consequent identification with the mother. That gives rise to the idea that the homosexual man loves his object in the same manner as he wishes to be loved by his mother. He is then said to deny his mother's lack of a penis on his own person and, owing to the threatening castration anxiety, can thus not bear the absence of the penis in the beloved object.

I hold the opinion that the incest wish does not succumb to repression, but rather that it fades completely into the background with the decline of the oedipal complex. The homosexual man loves those characteristics and traits in his love object which he rediscovers as his own in the other person. His partner has the same sexual characteristics as he himself because the sexual characteristics of the other sex trigger no erotic feelings in him. The assumption that the lack of such a heterosexual erotic attraction is evidence for a repression of these feeling is just as nonsensical as would be the assertion that every heterosexual male does not feel attracted by other males because he is repressing his unconscious homosexual tendencies. It is truer by far that all people are subject to sexual excitation only under quite specific circumstances, and that they do not respond erotically at all in most contacts with others. In that regard, there is certainly no difference between heterosexuals and homosexuals.

As soon as neurotic disturbances occur in love relationships, the circumstances change, with heterosexuals as well as with homosexuals. Then it is entirely possible that a man's identification with his mother will result in the fact that he loves the woman he chooses, or the man he finds homosexually attractive, in the same manner he wishes to be loved by his mother. Unconscious motives may force him to deny his mother's lack of a penis with the help of his own person, but to turn sexually to women anyway. In the sexual act, he provides the woman with his own penis and in that manner illusionarily denies her own lack of a penis.

In neurotic homosexuals, finally, things are often just as traditional opinion has recognized them to be. The neurotic disturbances that may occur in the development into homosexuality are often traceable to a more or less pronounced failure in the oedipal development. Pathological fixations result in regressions that are mainly related to the anal-sadistic or phallic-narcissistic stage of libido development. With a anal-sadistic regression, the oedipal child came to grief during the phallic phase, because during the discovery of the sexual characteristics, the child never succeeded in achieving a reality-related interpretation of the two faces of the parental figures. The consequence is an intense identification with the parent of the opposite sex. One may, then, in the case of a man, justifiably speak of an identification with the mother, or, in the case of a woman, of an identification with the father. Everything connected with the sexual differentiation of the sexes is interpreted regressively in the sense of omnipotence–impotence, and the attitude towards the surrounding world reflects, or exceeds, the societally predelineated overevaluation of polar pairs. The tendency characterized by a clinging to magical thinking aims at keeping the form of the sexual ideational representatives undefined. The behavior of such persons is disturbed. The opinions they hold seem undifferentiated. The man is of a particular effeminacy, the woman of a mask like stiffness in her behavior, as if she demonstrated, in everything she encounters, the degradation of women imposed by society.

In a phallic-narcissistic regression, the oedipal child came to grief at the point of overcoming the oedipal conflict. The discovery of the sexual characteristics of the parental figures did not result in a dedramatization of the castration anxiety because the interpretation of these characteristics, which was permeated by fantasies, could not be replaced by an interpretation adjusted to reality. With the oedipal boy, the idea of the penis was tied up with the feared aggression of the father and constantly maintained the quality of a penis of dispute. Sexual activity is thus used for the channeling of aggressive impulses and serves almost exclusively a fantasized increase in power in sexual and societal areas. With the oedipal girl, owing to the phallic, illusionary processing, the female sexual characteristics experience something powerfully absorbing and devouring, which is continuously mixed into the behavior of the subsequently homosexual woman and serves, as in the man, a fantasized increase in power in the sexual and societal realms. The behavior of these people is disturbed. They tend towards inconsiderate and blackmailing sexual relationships and they despise their sexual partners. Apparently, certain male and female prostitutes are recruited from this neurotic type, who in their behavior with their sexual partners act out in caricature, as it were, the exploitative conditions of our society.

OBSERVATIONS CONCERNING EVENTS IN PUBERTY AND ADULTHOOD

The discovery of the head of Janus with the two faces of the parental figures, which dedramatizes and thus terminates the oedipal conflict at its apex, pales, together with infantile instinctiveness, during the latency period. During puberty, sexuality increases dramatically and expresses itself in the homosexual object choice, which is in obvious contradiction with the moral demands of the prevailing societal conditions. At first, homosexuals cannot get their bearings in their environment. Also, there is no place provided for them. They are imperceptibly isolated and discriminated against, and, accordingly, they feel disturbed in their self-esteem. Often they become vulnerable, unstable, and anxious. The problems they face are involved with the "coming out" of homosexuality (Dannecker and Reiche, 1974, p. 23ff., 67ff., 331). Coming out represents a process in which homosexuals consciously recognize and reveal themselves as such. This process discloses how and to what extent the direct confrontation of homosexuality with the internalized image of one's own person, on the one hand, and, on the other, with the realities of society, is or is not possible.

The greatest stresses to which homosexuals are exposed originate from the society in which they live. These stress conditions are not easily surveyed and, in any event, cannot be explained solely by the discrimination to which homosexuals are subjected by society. Wherever homosexuality is rigorously suppressed and forbidden, social circumstances exist in which the life of the individual is particularly subjected to control by society. The anxiety about homosexuality prevailing in these societies can easily be recognized in that anxiety's violent defenses. These can be traced back to superego contents that reject instinctuality per se as something dangerous. Similar anxieties impel large segments of the white society of the United States to interpret the problem of the blacks as a danger threatening from some unrestrained sexual instinctuality in these people, who in reality are fighting for their equal social rights. Equally absurd are the anxieties about homosexuals in those places where the interests of individuals are subordinated to a higher social aim, where, that is, certain goals are achieved more effectively in groups than would be the case through individual initiatives in competitive struggle. In addition to all military organizations, these include educational institutions, youth organizations, clubs, unions, professional associations, and many more; in these institutions homosexuality poses such insoluble problems that it is denied, eliminated, forbidden, or suppressed by means of hostility and discrimination. The worldwide, stereotypical defense reactions against homosexuality express the fear that the assumed instinctuality of homosexuals might lead to an increase in homosexual autonomy that society can no longer tolerate. With regard to the realistic societal effects, this unconscious interpretation of the "homosexual danger" is absurd. With regard, however, to the inner-psychic function that homosexuality has in the homosexual's love life, it is intuitively correct. These conditions are confusing to homosexuals, since the society in which they customarily live imputes to them a sexual role they do not possess, the role, that is, of the unrestrained, instinctual androgyne. They are, however, no more instinctual than heterosexuals, and also no more unrestrained. Their sexual role, though different from that of heterosexuals is defined. To define that role for themselves, to form it, and to maintain it is the primary problem confronting the adult homosexual, and it also represents the primary area of confrontation with society. It is, in fact, a process of consciousness, representing the third turning of the switches in the development into homosexuality.

The sexual role of the adult develops out of the oedipal heritage. In heterosexuals, the expectations emanating from society and the image formed by the individual of his or her role as man or woman generally correspond. The difference in anatomic sexual characteristics makes it possible to rationalize the patterns of behavior and experience that are determined by polar contrasts and emphasize the differences between man and woman in all respects. The sexual role of homosexuals is defined differently. The image the male homosexual forms about his masculinity, or the homosexual woman about her femininity, is determined by exchangeable and alternating patterns of behavior, and by experiences that do not emphasize the difference between man and woman but, rather, secure autonomy and independence in the sexual life. Also heterosexuals strive for autonomy and independence in their sexual lives, but only secondarily. The precondition for them is self-confirmation as a man or as a woman. Homosexuals also want to confirm themselves as men or women, but only secondarily. For them the precondition is knowing that they are sexually autonomous and independent.

It is important to homosexuals not to appear maladjusted and out of touch with reality. Thus they have to, and want to, adapt. In adapting, they are subject to the societal compulsion to interpret all socially and societally effective aspects according to the model of pairs of polar opposition. They are thus in danger of orienting their love lives according to this point of view. If they fall into these snares, the alternating role-play in their sexual behavior becomes so impaired that their ability to love is disturbed. Many otherwise healthy homosexuals yield to the pressure of these norms of society. This happens mainly through an escape in two directions, which also indicate the direction in which neurotic disturbances may develop.

One escape exists in the fact that they can no longer become seriously involved with a partner, because numerous societally significant qualities, such as professional position, societal influence, possessions, esteem, power, and so forth, bring up polar contrasts to an unbearable extent. This sets up severe aggressions in the relationship with the partner. Homosexuals often give way to such a development and begin seeking sexual gratification in their own anonymity with partners who remain as anonymous as they. The resulting distortion of their love life — a distortion that is due to the pressures of society and not to a primarily conditioned, infantile regression — results in an ever more frequent change of partners and ever more fleeting encounters. That is at least one of the causes for the promiscuity in the homosexual subculture.

The other escape, which many otherwise healthy homosexuals choose, is the refuge found with certain members of the family. Thus the homosexual man often lives with his mother or sister, the homosexual woman with her father or brother. Although these family members feel odd about the homosexuality of their child or sibling, tender connections in the background manage to moderate the pressure of societal norms. The assumption of classical theory that precisely this withdrawal of homosexuals to their own small families proves the fixation of incestuous relationships, is often refuted in practice by psychoanalytic experience. The assumption may indeed be correct in the case of a severe neurotic development. In many cases, however, it is a supposition. It is apparent, in fact, that relatively healthy homosexuals can leave their family members without any conflict when an uncovering and working through of the unconscious pressure of societal behavior patterns is made possible in the analytic interpretation process. This permits an adjustment and a new orientation, with the result that homosexuals then adapt their behavior to society, while still organizing their love lives autonomously.

One might assume that the inner-psychic disposition of homosexuals to move flexibly from one role-behavior into another would find expression not only in their sexual life but also, quite generally, in their attitude towards society. This would imply a critical attitude towards society, going beyond efforts to attain equal rights and be recognized, which would have the consequence of a revolt against the inflexibility and compulsion of societal structures. Although there are notable exceptions, the great majority of homosexuals is neither socially critical nor politically interested. Even where homosexuals appear as closed groups in the institutions of their subculture, they do not constitute any danger to society. So far, no explosive revolutionary energy has emanated from them. In their institutions, they usually copy and emulate bourgeois behavior patterns and tend to regard themselves as objects of the consumer society.

When considering in which countries a homosexual subculture exists and in which countries it does not, one might think that a private-enterprise, capitalistic society would provide the most fertile ground for the spread of homosexuality. Even though this thesis seems to provide a plausible explanation for the rigorous suppression of homosexuality in the Soviet Union, Cuba, and China, it must be firmly contradicted, for it merely expresses a rationalization. Where homosexuality is punishable by death (Libya, Argentina) or by concentration camp (Cuba), or simply denied and declared nonexistent (China), and also where homosexuality is tolerated but pushed into a ghettolike subculture and neutralized, it is an underground threat emanating from homosexuality that is the cause of these direct and indirect repressive measures. The threat, so difficult to comprehend, arises from the latent, potentially available revolt always manifested by homosexuals when they feel restricted in their need for autonomy. This need is so closely connected to their sexual organization that even a slight restriction, which would not at all hinder others in their ability to love, may release unpredictable reactions in homosexuals. If they were to appear as a homogeneous group, homosexuals would have the effect of embodying a dangerously high degree of autonomy, so that one spark, jumping over from their sexual organization to their environment, would suffice to explode the powder keg of dammed-up aggressions in the respective prevailing society. Unconsciously, homosexuals may contribute to this effect, but they are not aware of it. The potential threat remains an illusion. But it has a feedback effect on the homosexuals, who often are plagued by persecution anxieties and paranoid fears. A far-reaching process is necessary to bring this anxiety, which originates from the fact that the environment senses them as a danger, into the consciousness of homosexuals. If the individual, or entire groups, were to succeed in cultivating this consciousness, one could probably expect, not a reconstitution of society but, rather, a better self-understanding on the part of homosexuals, through which their influence on the environment would be more revolutionary in many respects than it may appear.

NEUROTIC DISTURBANCES IN A DEVELOPMENT INTO HOMOSEXUALITY, AND GUIDELINES FOR A PSYCHOTHERAPEUTIC APPROACH

One can speak of a psychosexual development into homosexuality only if the turning of the switches occurred at the three stations I have described, and if what is characteristic for homosexuals has been structurally integrated into their personality. As I have emphasized repeatedly, the same-sex object choice, so easily visible, must not be equated with the personality structure responsible for it. Far more characteristic are the psychosexual modes of experience I have described, which are integrated free of conflict and exchanged alternatingly, and can shift pleasurably from one role behavior into the other. I have also pointed out that this flexibility and elasticity represents an inner-psychic disposition that must not be understood to include all traits, particularly not social adaptation, but, rather, determines very specifically the conditions of erotization and of the homosexuals' capacity and capability for sexual experience. The neurotic disturbances that may emerge in the development into homosexuality indicate structural defects, distortions, inhibitions, or excessive instinctual reactions that damage, more or less decisively (reversibly or irreversibly), this slowly developing inner-psychic disposition. We can differentiate three types of harmful influences that can make homosexuals sick.

(1) If the preoedipal development, with its typical intensification of the significance of autoerotism and its the functional change described above, was not sufficient to round out the coherence within the narcississtic realm, instability and an increased vulnerability will remain extant. This expresses itself in a narcissistic disturbance.

(2) If, at the apex of the oedipal phase, the autoerotic activities of the child are frustrated or halted by the parents with crudely sexualized or aggressive reactions, the oedipal complex will usually not be dedramatized by the new cathexis of the gender differences. Since the image of the sexual being can then no longer be separated from the characteristics of the sexual role, the subsequent homosexual object choice is deeply disturbed.

(3) If, during the coming out of homosexuality and later on, modes of behavior and experience delineated by society determine the homosexual's sex life to a large degree, an intolerance towards one's own homosexuality develops, which will result in depressive states with self-destructive tendencies, psychosomatic disturbances, and irritations tinged with aggression.

In principle, homosexuals who seek counseling or psychological or medical treatment require that the counselor or therapist accommodate them to a certain degree, that is, diagnose them, for the moment, as homosexuals who are as healthy as possible, not as sick as possible. Therefore, every therapist or counselor should assume that the crisis in which these homosexuals find themselves must be understood as a critical situation in life; that is, the therapist should not try to explain the disturbances and not, by hauling in the fate the instincts suffered in early childhood. Under our societal and cultural conditions, the development of a crisis in homosexuals is primarily and most frequently caused by the effects of disputes with society, by unresolved conflicts during the coming-out phase, and by painful setbacks in interhuman relationships in day-to-day living. Unfortunately, the milieu of the homosexual subculture often copies the patterns of behavior and experiences predelineated by society and thus actually intensifies the most frequent disturbances confronting homosexuals, instead of alleviating them. However, in some countries there are remarkable exceptions.

Of secondary importance, but still relatively frequent, are neurotic disturbances in homosexuals that can be traced back to the oedipal conflict.

Lastly, and relatively seldom, deep-seated narcissistic defects may be the focal point of a homosexual's psychopathology.

Homosexuals with crisis-ridden developments, who belong to the last two groups named, should be treated by a psychoanalyst, whereas the large group of those mentioned first could be made aware of the origins of their disturbances by nonanalytic therapists and counselors and could be encouraged to stand up for what they are without feeling disqualified, sick, or more neurotic than others.

It is of decisive importance for all counselors, physicians, psychotherapists, and psychoanalysts to meet the homosexual as a partner whose experience of psychosexual development is as justified, and must be taken just as seriously, as the therapist's own. However, if counselors, physicians, psychotherapists, or psychoanalysts believe they want to, or even are able to, "cure" homosexuals of their homosexuality, they abuse their societal prestige for manipulatory purposes. If they are convinced of their point of view, and if they manage to convince the homosexual that he or she can be "cured," they are succumbing to an illusion, for they are restricting the autonomous functions of that person in a damaging manner by means of their influence upon him or her. Everyone has an influence over others. It certainly is not this characteristic which distinguishes the counselor, physician, psychotherapist, or psychoanalyst.

Counselors and therapists can help homosexuals only if they understand and bring to light the causes of the difficulties. If they can do that, the homosexual will be able to arrange his love life, for the first time or again, in a manner suitable not to the counselor or therapist but to himself. The theory of psychoanalytic technique describes a number of concepts that help the analyst avoid the snares that may hinder the analytic process with a homosexual analysand (Morgenthaler, 1978).

For orienting oneself in counseling and therapy, the fine details of the technical concepts of psychoanalysis are probably less important than the fact that numerous formations of homosexual modes of experience and homosexual activities may also figure in those people with neurotic disturbances who are not homosexuals, because they have not gone through a development into homosexuality. If, for instance, oedipal development miscarries in a heterosexual, regressive processes may result in an overcathexis of autoerotic positions that provide opportunity for compulsive homosexual phantasies or activities and are experienced as torment. Such developments may make use of the reactivation of autoerotic strivings during various phases of the libidinal development and apply homosexual inclinations as bridging modalities. Most forms of latent homosexuality in heterosexuals can be placed in this classification, and can be influenced by working them through psychoanalytically. They can be influenced because they are symptoms and because they have little to do with a development into homosexuality. Conversely, there are developments in homosexuals that, for neurotic reasons, enforce heterosexual fantasies and activities that are experienced as tormenting because they originate from an anal-retentive mode of experience. Also these neurotic disturbances can be influenced in psychoanalytic treatment.

Furthermore, homosexual inclinations are apparent as secondary manifestations in almost all perversions. In those cases, the homosexual inclinations represent processes that perverts experience in such a way as to make them venture into object relationships not limited to inanimate objects; this is achieved by an increase in autoerotic cathexes, in accordance with the ideal image of the own person. This applies in particular to one group often equated with homosexuals—the sadomasochists, who have a special preference for leather, iron rings, and steel belts, and who discharge their perversion through homosexual practices. Fetishists, transvestites, and other perverts make use of homosexual activities to lend their perversion a livelier sheen than it would otherwise have.

Overall, the conditions I have described in the development into homosexuality, and their demarcation from the development into heterosexuality, are never so sharply defined or so one-sided. Sexual activity and partner choice are in no way directed so entirely at either one or the other practice as is generally assumed. There are men who are not homosexual but who prefer to develop relationships with homosexual women, and vice versa. There are comparatively many homosexuals who also enter into heterosexual relationships. Because this is known, people like to talk about bisexuality in such cases. That term merely veils the impossibility of maintaining any polarization in the field of sexuality. There is, in fact, no such thing as hetero-, homo-, or bisexuality. There is only sexuality, which, along extremely varied lines of development, ultimately finds a specific form of expression for each individual.

7

SEXUALITY AND PSYCHOANALYSIS

What we call the sexual is instinctuality expressed in instinctual impulses. Instinctual impulses—undefinable by their very nature—follow the "primary process," which psychoanalysis rightfully consigns to the id. Freud, who was most profoundly convinced of the incomprehensibility of the id, makes use of metaphorical paraphrases in his presentation.

> The id is the dark, inaccessible part of our personality; what little we know of it we have learned from our study of dream-work and of the construction of neurotic symptoms, and most of that . . . can be described only as a contrast to the ego. We approach the id with analogies: we call it a chaos, a cauldron full of seething excitations. . . . It is filled with energy reaching it from the instincts, but it has no organization, produces no collective will, but only the striving to bring about the satisfaction of the instinctual needs subject to the observance of the pleasure principle. The logical laws of thought do not apply in the id, and this is true above all of the law of contradiction. Contrary impulses exist side by side, without cancelling each other out or diminishing each other: at the most they may converge to form compromises under the dominating economic pressure towards the discharge of energy. . . . There is nothing in the id that corresponds to the idea of time; there is no recognition of the passage of time. . . . The id of course knows no judgements of value, no good and evil, no morality. The economic or, if you prefer, the quantitative factor, which is intimately linked to the pleasure principle, dominates all its processes. Instinctual cathexes seeking

discharge—that, in our view, is all there is to the id. It even seems that the energy of these instinctual impulses is in a state different from that in the other regions of the mind, far more mobile and capable of discharge; otherwise the displacements and condensations would not occur which are characteristic of the id and which so completely disregard the quality of what is cathected—what in the ego we should call an idea [Freud, 1933, pp. 73-75].

This text makes it clear how difficult things become when one gets involved with the id. Freud applies comparisons used by the dominator to describe those who are hard to dominate. He states very impressively that the instinctual impulses in the id are completely incomprehensible when he says "that the energy of these instinctual impulses is in a state different from that in the other regions of the mind." The difficulty of becoming involved with the id is to be found above all in the fact that the aimlessness of the primary-process instinctual impulses contradicts our need to think logically. If we insist that the instinctual impulses in the id cannot be defined because of their aimlessness, then there are contradictions in the text quoted insofar as the instinctual impulses in the id are assigned certain aims, ideational contents, and comprehensible psychic processes, even though they are in all cases unconscious. When Freud says that the id strives to bring about the satisfaction of the instinctual needs subject to the pleasure principle, he assigns the instinctual impulses of the id an aim, namely the compliance with the pleasure principle. I am of the opinion that it would be much more consistent to say that the events of the primary process in the ego or its preliminary stages take shape in the pursuit of the pleasure principle. The pursuit of a principle, be it the reality principle or the pleasure principle, can originate only in another region of the mind, that is, in the ego or its preliminary stages, but never in the id, for there is nothing but aimless potential dynamics within the primary process. I conclude from this that the difficulty in approaching the id results, again and again, in the projective displacing into the id of processes that the ego develops under the influence of the primary process. That seems to me also to be the case when Freud assumes that contrary impulses in the id, under the dominating economic pressure towards a discharge of energy, may converge to form compromises. I am of the opinion that contrary impulses cannot exist in the id and that compromise formations can emerge only in the ego. The same holds true for displacements and condensations.

When we speak of the sexual, in contrast to organized sexuality, we mean by that the instinctuality of the id, that is, an energetic potential that gives experience in general an urgelike dimension. Instinctual impulses are undirected, goalless, timeless, unconditioned, and, in particular, unconscious. The only thing we can say about them has to do with their tendency — the tendency of the instinctual impulses is motion that becomes visible and perceptible in emotionality. With its emotional content, the instinctual motion of the primary process resonates in everything we do, in every gesture, every thought, in everything we communicate and everything we experience. That alone makes us appear alive. Even at this moment, as you read this text, the primary-process background is just as important for what I want to communicate as is the written, perceptible content.

Psychoanalysis recognized these conditions early on, but it describes them not as the expression of the sexual but as what it calls transference. Every time a transference develops, primary-process events are involved on both sides. They are felt, but all too easily overlooked. However, we may say that in the transference the sexual appears in an already organized form — the erotic cathexes — in addition to finding expression in a specific mode of perception. This mode of perception is instinctual in the sense of the primary process and is connected with the emotional movement in which both partners in the psychoanalytic relationship find themselves. It is unconscious and distinct from the other, the conscious mode of perception, which is connected with the tangible, the learnable and comprehensible, and which makes use of all the aids available in logical thinking, in speech and in writing, and in precise observation and interpretation.

Of the two modes of perception, psychoanalysis, like the sciences in general, rests on the one as a principle and places the other in the background as something difficult to grasp and, in a certain sense, disreputable. It is difficult indeed to disregard that one is oneself constantly subject to the primary process. We always need both perceptual modalities in order to perceive our own reality and that of others. Psychoanalysis does not underestimate these conditions. It assigns the primary-process perception its proper place in the development of transference and countertransference; but then it speaks of intuition, empathy, free-floating attention, creativity, and experience of the personal analysis of the analyst as though these were characteristics or properties favoring the primary-process capability of perception. In my opinion, these terms are defined much too narrowly. Everyone is intuitive, empathic, compassionate, and we all have access to creative powers.

It is not a question of which intuitive, empathic, creative forces a person must develop in order to be capable of following the primary-process mode of perception. Everyone follows it. In our cultural realm it is, so it appears, harmoniously built into the structure of secondary-process perception. The price for that is that the disharmony between primary and secondary process must be made unconscious. With that, however, the instinctually sexual closeness inherent in every interpersonal contact and relationship also remains unconscious. An experience from our ethnopsychoanalytic research activities (see Parin, Morgenthaler, and Parin-Matthey, 1963), will show how this disharmony can manifest itself.

To begin with, the primary-process quality of being available for emotional response accounts for the attunement of the individual. It is humane-specific and independent of social and cultural backgrounds and therefore immediately perceptible and comprehensible. It is quite different with the mood of the moment. That is determined by affects brought into action and controlled by the ego. Since the ego organization and its structures follow a developmental process that must take social and cultural institutions into consideration, the mood of a person, for instance one from a foreign culture, is by no means as evident as the person's attunement.

In Africa and Papua, New Guinea, we have repeatedly had the same experience during our ethnopsychoanalytic research: with regard to the emotional attunement, our partner from the foreign culture was always familiar, intimate, and transparent to us and we to him. However, as for our affective states concerning the objects and the attitudes towards ourselves and the goals of our activities, we often faced our partner—and he us—as if confronting a riddle.

The generally comprehensible, immediately perceptible in the other person represents the instinctual impulses of the primary process that find their expression in the emotional movement. The other impression, sometimes unempathic and confusing, is the consequence of the events in the secondary process.

In order to clarify what I mean by a disharmony between the primary and the secondary process, I must address the ego, the instance of the psyche embodying the reality principle and mediating between the inner and the outer world. The ego is under the influence of the events of the primary process. These events are embodied in the ego, to begin with, in the pursuit of the pleasure principle. The influence of the primary process is organized and structured during the course of the development of the ego and the libido. The instinctual impulses are directed into specific tracks and express themselves as wishes pressing towards gratification. Demands for gratification are subject to conditions, have consequences, and effect defenses. In the ego, temporal processes, qualitative valuations, and quantitative standards channel the events of the primary process towards the events of the secondary process. The events of the secondary process direct their attention primarily towards the absorption of the emotional movement emanating from the primary process. Only secondarily, through the formation of relevant concepts, is the secondary process also put into the service of the reality principle.

To illustrate what I mean by saying that the events of the secondary process primarily direct their attention towards absorption of the movement emanating from the primary process, let me use the analogy of a vehicle, the design of which is determined essentially by its capacity to absorb the anticipated speed the vehicle is capable of achieving. If we compare car and airplane from this point of view, it is mainly a question of the undercarriage, which has to be constructed differently in each of them. In the automobile, a chassis, a suspension of the wheels with springs and shock absorbers, and a steering mechanism are necessary to control and absorb the motions the vehicle is expected to encounter. With the airplane, aerodynamic considerations become so important that the entire undercarriage has to comply to it. Everything is calculated in such a way that the airplane will absorb the movement that it may encounter at the enormous speeds it attains. Consequently, this is a matter of formal and structural given conditions that are determining factors in the construction and are in direct relationship with the stresses the vehicle experiences through the motion to which it is subjected.

The situation is similar to the function of the events of the secondary process. It is primarily a question of its formal and structural given conditions, which must absorb and keep under control the movement of the primary process with its undirected instinctual impulses of the id. Just as it is with vehicles, where all body parts can be developed only secondarily and according to the fundamental structures, so it is with ideational contents of every sort, whether conscious or unconscious, which disguise the formal and structural factors of the secondary process and depict it as something that is only *seemingly* harmonious in its merging with the emotional experiences of the primary process. In fact, however, one can never speak of a harmony between primary and secondary process.

The example of the vehicles is intended to show that the secondary disguise—interior installations and body parts—communicates to the driver and passengers the impression that they can master and control the motion to which they are subjected just as much as if they were moving without technical means. By analogy, conscious and unconscious ideational contents of every kind, but also the becoming conscious of wishes, of needs, and of defense mechanisms against them, are those formations of the secondary process which communicate to us the impression that the vehemence of the primary-process instincts in the id could combine harmoniously with our modes of experience. In reality, the primary process in its motion is incompatible with the secondary process and its rigid, multilayered organizational system. The contradiction between the two is irrefutable. The disharmony is obvious. The primary process is mainly determined by the undirectedness of the instinctual impulses belonging to the id, whereas the secondary process guides all instinctuality into tracks, organizes it, and arranges it according to aims to which one must aspire.

When we speak of sexuality in contrast to that which is sexual, we are referring to what the secondary process has made of the instinctual impulses in the id. For what does it mean when we speak of a sexual instinct, of sexual instinct impulses that press for satisfaction, of a sexual object that is cathected? Could that be an expression of instinctuality?

I do not believe that it is; I think, rather, that this is the dictatorship of sexuality, established by the instinctual and ego developments by means of the events in the secondary process in order to absorb the motion of the primary process, guide it into certain controllable channels, and restrict it by means of conditions. Between the instinctual impulses of the primary process and this sexual dictatorship there exists a disharmony, which constitutes the difference between that which is sexual and that which we call sexuality.

Sexuality, in all its forms, is the result of a complicated, multilayered secondary process in which the instincts subordinate themselves to the extent that they express themselves in a directly sexual fashion. The potential of the instincts that escape the secondary-process channelization remains constantly available, free-floating, in order to admix itself, momentarily and reversibly, as an emotional movement to all sorts of ego functions.

Within the libido and ego developments, one can observe how the first steps towards the organization of the sexual occur. Erogenous zones are libidinally cathected, whereby specific ego functions provide these cathexes with fixed meanings. The oral cathexis modality, for instance, involves incorporation, anal retention and relaxation, phallic looking and showing, and conquest. These developmental results are the first organizational elements and structures of the secondary process that separate sexuality from the instinctual impulses of the primary process.

Instinctual impulses are, as it were, recruited in the id and disciplined to ego-syntonic functions. By marching in step with the libido and ego developments, they learn the rifle drill of wish formation that presses towards satisfaction. Targets are set up and must be aimed at. These are the objects that from now on are cathected with the energy of the instincts.

In our society the individual is subject to the dictatorship of a sexual organization that continually seeks perfection. It is comparable to a society ruled, for example, by a military power. In corporal structure and biology, everything is preplanned. During the phallic-narcissistic phase of libido development, when one's own sexual organs are highly cathected for the first time and the child's first love relationship is about to take place, sexuality attains its lasting home in the center of the psychic living space. The genitals are this living space. Just as the population under a military power follows orders in a more or less disciplined fashion, the individual more or less voluntarily follows conditions determined by sexual organization. Our ethnopsychoanalytic research in Africa and Melanesia has shown that the dictatorship of sexuality affects the emotional experiences of the individual according to the culturally conditioned process of socialization. Also the relationship between ego and id arranges itself in accordance with a society's form of government. This is connected with the conditions under which the secondary process develops in early childhood, step by step and alternating with epigenetic crises. As Spitz (1965) and others have shown, the mother communicates to her infant the deportments and attitudes required by society through the manner in which she deals with the infant. This influence effects the culturally specific, societally adequate formation of the secondary process, which channels and organizes, step by step and phase-specifically, the instinctual impulses of the primary process.

Among peoples of other cultures the disharmony between the events of the secondary process and the aimless instinctual impulses of the primary process does not necessarily take the same form as in our own society, for which the comparison of the dictatorship of sexuality with that of a military junta seems justified, in view of the hostility of our industrial societies towards instinct. With this comparison I do not want to claim that sexuality plays only this role in our life. I intentionally chose a point of view from which the harmony between instinct and sexuality may be questioned, and which should show that the relationship between love and sexuality is not a simple, smooth one, but rather that both oppose each other in a ruptured relationship from the very beginning.

Love can develop only if the instinctual impulses of the primary process have open access to sexuality. For a variety of reasons, this is not simply a matter of course. Since the secondary process is organized by means of the ego and libido developments, and expands the instinctual impulses into a dictatorship, situations arise in which the instinctual impulses of the primary process may be blocked to a higher or lesser degree. As a matter of fact, the secondary process produces a series of organizing factors during the development of sexuality, of which I want to emphasize two, since their reciprocal effect on each other has a retroactive effect on the primary process.

One of the organizers is the *compulsion to repeat,* to which the sexual object cathexis is subjected and which represents an immediate consequence of the channelization of primary-process instinctual impulses into sexual object cathexes. The other concerns the *dependency on the sexual object,* which the secondary process extorts from the individual's infantile developmental history.

THE REPETITION COMPULSION
IN SEXUAL OBJECT CATHEXIS

Freud speaks of the unconscious repetition compulsion, which he ascribed to the conservative nature of the instincts. "It seems, then, that an instinct is an urge inherent in organic life to restore an earlier state of things" (Freud, 1920, p. 36). In the "New Introductory Lectures on Psycho-Analysis" (1933, p. 106), Freud acknowledges that the compulsion to repeat even vaults over the pleasure principle and can lead some people to repeat and repeat, uncorrected, the described reactions to their own detriment. Out of these considerations Freud then came to assume a death instinct.

In the development of psychoanalytic theory, the assumption of a death instinct was rejected decades ago as misleading and fruitless. I mention these connections here merely to show that this is quite obviously a point of view one uses to understand a specific psychic phenomenon. The point of view that Freud chose in this connection could not lead any further. What was Freud's point of view?

To answer that question, let me quote Freud himself again, even though he did not, in fact, write the following in the context mentioned above, but rather in his observation of hunger and thirst as instinctual impulses: "A good part of the confusing impression made by all this is that we have not given separate consideration to the alteration which the influence of the organized ego makes in the instinctual impulses that belonged originally to the id. We find ourselves on firmer ground when we investigate the manner in which the life instinct serves the sexual function" (Freud, 1933, pp. 97–98).

Freud's point of view concentrated on how the instinctual life was expressed in the ego and thus in sexuality. Psychoanalysis, incidentally, has always insisted on understanding everything psychic from the point of view of the secondary process. That is absolutely understandable, for no rational theory can be constructed from the point of view of the primary process.

I represent a different point of view, and I focus my observation on the change the instinctual impulses undergo under the influence of the organized ego. I do not abandon the basis of psychoanalysis in my conception, I merely assert that the definition of instinct as an urge to restore an earlier state can only be valid for the sexual instinctuality already organized in the life of the mind, but by no means for the events of the primary process, since instinctuality is identical with emotionality within the events of the primary process. This instinctual aspect of the primary process provides the attunement of the individual; it is free-floating vitality. The only thing urgent in the events of the primary process is that which is alive, maintained, and intended to continue. One definitely must not speak of a compulsion to repeat or of an observance of the pleasure principle within the events of the primary process, since neither aim nor conditions or time exist there. The mark of the primary process is its aimlessness. The aimlessness is what drives to seek the new. Without this impetus, there would be, just as in the secondary process, nothing but repetitions; and if there were nothing but repetitions, there would be no past, and also no history. The aimlessness of the primary process is the true creative aspect in life. The compulsion to repeat is always a matter of the secondary process.

The instinctual impulses, recruited and disciplined by the developmental processes of the ego organization, remain lastingly tied to the primary process—in spite of their secondary-process—structuring, and they press towards a free-floating aimlessness. Their activity as organized sexual instincts somehow seems constantly forced, seems to be missing the point. If the instinctual tension has achieved its goal, it immediately increases again in order to aspire towards the restoration of the earlier, original state, that is, the state in which the instinctual impulses were located in the primary process. The increase of instinctual tension is aimed at breaking through the secondary process of the sexual organization, which actually can succeed only if the ego structures are deficient and if the tracks laid by the secondary process lose their function. This indicates that such a breakthrough would in no way be desirable, for it would bring the individual into a psychopathological situation where he or she would be helplessly exposed to the instincts.

I want to emphasize once more that the point of view I choose derives from the examination of the changes that the instinctual impulses, originally belonging to the id, experience under the influence of the organized ego. During this examination I have come to the conclusion that the repetition compulsion in the sexual object cathexis is caused by the dictatorship of sexuality and is established by the ego organization.

This dictatorship of sexuality is the inevitable result of the libido and ego developments. Thus, obviously, removing the dictatorship is not the issue. The problem resulting from the disharmony between the primary-process instinctual impulses and the dictatorship of sexuality—or, in other words, between the sexual and sexuality—is rooted elsewhere.

THE DEPENDENCY ON THE SEXUAL OBJECT

We can come to agreeable terms with the urgency of the instinctual impulses of the primary process, for it is fun to give way to them over and over again. It is otherwise with the repetition compulsion in the sexual cathexis, for it represents the consequence of a throttling of the aimless instinctual impulses of the primary process, which should have free access to sexuality. With the appearance, in the sexual object cathexis, of the compulsion to repeat, insurmountable conflicts may well emerge, because the sexual development, no matter what type it may be, necessarily induces dependency on the sexual object.

Man comes into this world like a premature baby and requires, as does no other form of life in nature, loving care and provision for many years. Biologically, human beings are dependent upon the providers to the extent that their entire lives are subject to this influence. In the course of early infantile development, the most important sexual object cathexis takes place during the oedipal phase. The sexual object cathexis is linked to the elementary dependency on the parent cathected. Subsequent to the oedipal phase, the latency period begins, in which no collision of the dependency on the sexual object with the repetition compulsion in the sexual cathexis arises. The overcoming of the oedipal complex is described by psychoanalysis as a process that I, from my chosen point of view, may describe as follows: The parent of the same sex introjects that psychical quality which imposes upon the individual from now on to cathect sexual objects that must not be identical with the objects upon which the child was unavoidably and vitally dependent. By the same token, the incest taboo, which is respected by all cultures, may be interpreted as a veto that concerns sexual relationships in which the repetition compulsion of the sexual cathexis forms a vicious circle with the dependency on the sexual object.

THE VICIOUS CIRCLE AND ITS
DISAVOWAL BY PSYCHOANALYTIC THEORY

I have spoken of a dictatorship of the sexuality in order to emphasize the forced and involuntary aspects that the sexual organization, with its built-in childhood fates of the instincts, imposes upon human experience. Only now does it become clear that the forced and rigid quality attached to sexuality is based on a deeply anchored linking of the sexual object cathexis with the dependency on the sexual object, a process that may subsequently result in a vicious circle if the urgency turns into compulsion and the dependency into a form of subjugation or enslavement. If this vicious circle does occur, an ego restriction with loss of the autonomous functions takes place, because the sexual object cathexis further deepens the dependency, and the dependency on the sexual object activates the sexual cathexis. The rigidity of the connection of cathexes and dependency, which is based on fixations and regressive repetitions, indicates the instinct-restricting and instinct-inhibiting functions of the secondary process functions, which may throttle, restrict, or even block the events of the primary process. The emotional movement emanating from the primary process has the task of connecting sexuality, in whatever state of development it may be and whatever definitive form it may take, with the ability to love. If in my sexual behavior I am forced by the sexual dictatorship, to which I more or less succumb, to fall into a subjugated dependency on the sexual object by reason of the developing vicious circle, a strangulation of the expressions of my emotional movement results. With the intensity of its energy, the primary process then bursts this strangulation, creating aggressions. Thus I come to the conclusion that the actual problem resulting from the disharmony between the primary process and the secondary process is a problem of aggression.

And with this I enter the field of the metapsychologically founded theory of aggression. I cannot share psychoanalytic theory's opinion that postulates an actual aggressive instinct supposedly present in the id, in the primary process. That standpoint once again introduces something qualitative, with specific aims, into the events of the primary process, which is completely foreign to its nature, since the instinctual impulses of the primary process are without direction, aimless, timeless, and deeply unconscious. The primary process is characterized by the emotional movement that strives for free access to all activities. If this access is strangled and blocked, the aimless instinctual impulses of the primary process are expressed as aggressive impulses. Psychoanalytic theory (see Rapaport, 1967) has ascribed to the instinctual impulses of the primary process the quality of undifferentiation and made the events of the secondary process, in interaction with the processes of maturing and developing, responsible for the function of differentiation, so that, for example, the undifferentiated instinctual parts of the id are said to obtain their mature and differentiated form of expression in the developed sexual organization. It is superfluous in this assumption to consider a disharmony between primary and secondary process.

In my opinion, psychoanalytic theory created a confusion when it disavowed this disharmony on the grounds of the so-called aggression instinct. That confusion is connected with the fact that aggression, in contrast to sexuality, knows no development. There is no development of aggression that would correspond to libido development. There also is no organization of aggression that would correspond to sexual organization. The actual domain of sexuality is the sexual organs and their functions. In comparison, aggression has no domain and is comparable to guerrillas: hidden somewhere, without defined function, and never capturable as a unit. It always appears when something or other gets strangled.

Aggression is the other expression of the primary process, which appears when the conditions in the ego develop in such a manner that the emotional movement is inhibited and disturbed in one way or another.

The question is under what conditions the emotional movement will become so disturbed or inhibited that the vicious circle described above materializes in the love life, and causes the aimless instinctual impulses of the primary process to become effective as agressions. One may also ask under what conditions the emotional movement emanating from the primary process connects sexuality with the capability to love. Although psychoanalytic theory poses the question differently, the explanations it offers may be formulated as follows.

The vicious circle is the consequence of a neurotic development with regressions and fixations resulting in an inability to overcome the oedipal complex, unless, of course, it is due to severe disturbances already existing in the ego development. The connection between sexuality and the capability to love follows the mastering of the oedipal complex and its decline, whereby the genital stage of the libido development is attained. It is thus the result of a maturing and developmental process.

In my opinion, this explanation is inadequate, because it does not take into account the disharmony that exists between the aimless instinctual drives of the primary process and the sexual organization of the secondary process. It would be as if this disharmony were the result of a neurotic development and were to become irrelevant upon the mastering of the oedipus complex and the attainment of genital primacy. Psychoanalytic theory has always neglected to observe as something separate the changes to which the instinctual impulses in the id are subjected under the influence of the organized ego; instead, it has been satisfied with regarding the instinctual drives of the primary process as undifferentiated, in order to ascribe the function of differentiation to the secondary process and its reciprocal interaction with development and maturing. I do not share this point of view, and I maintain that love and sexuality, from the very beginning, are facing each other within a ruptured relationship.

THE DISHARMONY BETWEEN PRIMARY AND SECONDARY PROCESS IN THE EXPERIENCE OF THE INDIVIDUAL AND IN SOCIETY

It is the instinctual destiny of every human being to develop a dependency on the love object when the sexual object cathexis remains preserved. In order to prevent the development of a vicious circle, certain attitudes and deportments develop unconsciously.

(1) I can attune myself as though sexuality played only a secondary role in my life. I deny the sexual and experience events of the primary process as something intellectually sublime, infusing into all my activities. Sexual cathexes and experiences, in my opinion, are auxiliary phenomena without any central significance. With this attitude, remarkable energies are bound up for the banishment and pacification of the sexual dictatorship. That can lead to an ego restriction that disconcerts and disturbs me in the motivation of my actions. This will become apparent primarily in my love relationships.

(2) I can acknowledge the central significance of sexuality in everything I undertake and experience, but I cannot perceive the contradiction existing between the primary-process events and the sexual dictatorship. I accept instinctuality as something disquieting, or, as Freud expressed it, as something demonic. It is as if the instinctual impulses of the primary process evoked the sexual dictatorship. I would experience the unconscious aspect of instinctuality as something primitive and undifferentiated and would ascribe a calming and protective role to everything that differentiates and organizes itself. In my love relationships it thus would be important that my social role in society be secured and that, with the help of the institutions, I can steer my love relationship onto solid tracks. In doing so, I hardly realize that the developing dependency on my love object is gradually and quite discreetly superseded by a dependency on my role in society and by certain institutions. The dictatorial aspect is now beyond me and it effects, often almost imperceptibly, something disharmonic within me. Love becomes habitual and shallow because everything becomes mere repetition.

(3) There may be phases in my life when I constantly perceive the disharmony, the contradiction between my sexuality and the aimless emotional movement wanting to address everything new, and recognize this disharmony as the actual source of my conflictual

inclination. Thus I am constantly at the mercy of the dictatorship of my sexuality, in a perpetual struggle to form my love relationships in such a way that they may continue. My life then often takes dramatic turns. Crises in which I am rigid and aggressive alternate with phases of creative peaks.

In the sexual life of the individual, this vicious circle is most easily avoided by withdrawing or repelling the sexual object cathexis. Another possibility would be to free the dependency of its sexual content, for instance by displacing it onto certain institutions in which one lives. Thus one no longer feels dependent upon the sexual object, but rather upon the social role one attains by maintaining the sexual cathexis.

Both possibilities are often used during the course of a lifetime, and just as often dropped again. However, it may also happen that some particular possibility proves especially effective and productive, and so will be retained for decades. In all instances, these modes of behavior have their roots in early childhood experiences of infantile sexuality, with their traumatic experiences, and in the fates of the instincts manifest in the sexual organization.

Not only the individual but also every culture has developed specific possibilities for handling the vicious circle. Institutions may apply this vicious circle as a motor for their own survival by freezing it, as it were, and conserving it instead of dissolving it. Our society, for instance, has formed institutions that permit individuals to displace their deep-rooted dependency on the sexual object to the outside and to delegate it to their progeny. The dependency on the sexual object is switched to a social dependency on the sexual role. Marriage, with the customary formation of a nuclear family, forces the sexual partners to submit to laws transforming the mutual dependency into a permanent condition which is difficult to dissolve and which, to a large extent, is estranged from sexuality. In our cultural milieu, we recognize a process in which dependency on the sexual object is replaced to a considerable extent by a dependency on possessions. The woman possesses the name of the husband and the children. The husband possesses the family and the means of subsistence, which he supplies. In this constellation, one fact should not be underestimated, namely, that the children, in their existential dependency on both parental figures, are the ideal objects onto which both sexual partners, man and woman, can delegate their mutual sexual dependency. In this manner, both manage to a certain degree to maintain the sexual cathexis and to estrange the dependency on the sexual object in such a way that the instinctual impulses of the primary process are not blocked. These will then be apparent primarily in the emotional expressions within the family group.

It is important to me to show that a love relationship will have symptomatic character when a lasting cathexis of the sexual object is possible only because the the constant danger of becoming dependent on the sexual object is repressed and undone, so to speak, by the reliance on societal institutions and the procreation of progeny.

In our ethnopsychoanalytic investigations of the Dogon, an African society, we discovered in the transference processes that the group-ego of the individual responded with anxiety to the deepening of a relationship between two persons. In such relationships, the cathecting of the group is always more important than the cathecting of the sexual object, so that a dependency on the sexual partner does not appear. The dependency remains a dependency on the group. The maintenance of the cathexis of the sexual object finds its expression in the great significance of the child for the man and the woman, despite the fact that the child is assigned to the extended family, that is, the group, and is, to a large extent, removed from parental influence. In this society, traditions are effective in creating structures that will not even permit the emergence of the vicious circle of a sexual cathexis and the dependency on the sexual object.

In Papua, New Guinea, we found conditions characterized by a very special sensitivization to the merest beginnings of such a vicious circle. Cathexis of the sexual object and dependency on it constantly disquiet everyone, triggering explosive aggressions. Brawls between man and wife are everyday concomitants in the life of people who cling with emotional vehemence to the cathexis of their sexual objects and cannot stand dependency on them. The animistic contents of their culture find their expression in a transvestite ritual in which sexual identity is diffused in mocking speeches and the participants perform obscene dances, whereas in everyday life any form of sexual exhibition is frowned upon. An extensive mythological system, guarded exclusively by the men, oversees and guides everything that happens in nature and society. The transvestite ritual, too, derives from that system. Wherever situations and feelings of dependency emerge, they are justified by the members of this society by means of this mythology.

THE PSYCHODYNAMICS OF
THE LOVE RELATIONSHIP

There is no love relationship without a dependency on the partner. This dependency is the precondition for a regression that relaxes the ego organization. That permits the readmittance of instinctual impulses from the id that previously had no access to sexuality, because the events of the secondary process had stifled the aimless impulses of the primary process.

Regressions of this type were designated by Kris (1952, p. 103) as regressions in the service of the ego. The attitude towards the love object can change only if new parts of the id instincts are admitted, since they alone lead to the discovery of new aspects and characteristics of the partner. These discoveries create new forms of regression, which in turn admit new id impulses. This oscillation process results in ever new transformations and in a further development of sexuality in the sense of approaching the aimlessness of the instinctual impulse of the primary process (Erdheim, 1982). Under those conditions it is possible to link the emotional movement emanating from the primary process with sexuality. Thus the capability to love emerges independent from the installed sexual organization, whether heterosexual, homosexual, or perverse.

The sexual organization gets shaken up during adolescence, in accordance with developmental conditions. New regressions in the service of the ego emerge and make a new access to the id impulses possible. This results in a new formulation of the sexual organization, which was strengthened during the latency period. The first result of this new formulation is genital sexuality, with which nothing has yet been said as to the direction in which the adult sexual organization may further develop. There are no reasons to assume that sexual development is completed after adolescence or later on in the life of the adult. Sexuality will further develop to the extent that it accepts new id impulses, and it can develop only to the extent that it accepts these new impulses (see Erdheim, 1982).

If the rigidity of the linking of sexual cathexis and dependency on the sexual object — which is due to the dictatorship of sexuality, that is, to the effects of the events of the secondary processes — is determined in such a way that regression blocks the instinctual impulses in the id by means of repression, the vicious circle described above will emerge, accompanied by all kinds of neurotic developments. If the vicious circle occurs under the pressure of a certain constellation in the course of adult life, there are many possibilities to overcome it again. However, if the vicious circle became installed during adolescence, the subsequent sexual organization, be it heterosexual, homosexual or perverse, becomes rigid.

In such neurotic developments the love relationship has symptomatic character; this means that the processlike oscillation between dependency, regression, and admittance to sexuality of new id parts is not at all, or only insufficiently, possible. Analytic experience shows that the process leading to the capability to love is a painful one, and is accompanied by the work of mourning. This is a process of consciousness, to be differentiated from the work of mourning in the case of object loss. The essential difference is that the love object is not lost but currently present, and that there can be no question of a separation because both partners will meet again and again and their sexual relationship will continue.

This process of consciousness is so painful because our experiences of early childhood have determined our unconscious sexual concepts. These experiences were feelings of desperation and helplessness whenever the bonding with the object and the satisfaction of needs in the mutual interdependency of mother and child were not so secure that both could feel taken care of and content. From this point of view, the capability to love is a fundamentally new experience in the sexual life of the adult, which does not repeat the early infantile modes of experience but rather replaces them. The first experience of this type arises as a new point of reference during adolescence and represents a new acquisition that will be of decisive importance for the subsequent development of the capability to love. If this development of the capability to love succeeds, sexuality begins to be more and more subject to the primacy of the primary process, which asserts its influence without direction, aimless, timeless, without conditions, and unconsciously: creates new aspects of experiencing; and knows no repetition.

Relating this to psychoanalysis, we are dealing with a process in which, on the basis of an agreement, a relationship is initiated that will gradually deepen and attain the character of a sexual cathexis during the development of transference. For what is really at the center of the analytic process is the aim to make it possible for the analysand to maintain the cathexis of the sexual object, by means of the test object in the person of the analyst, and to overcome the dependency on the analyst—that is, to attain the ability to love.

THE HETEROSEXUAL CAPABILITY TO LOVE

People find their way amid their environment only if they can form a sense of identity, if they know who they are. The formation of this sense of identity is attached to the secondary process. It is obvious that the sense of identity should take on the dominating role in sexual life, since it alone enables the individual to take everything that is available from bodily structure, sexual organs, and societal institutions and use it—unexamined and, it would seem, harmoniously—to shape his sexual life. This constitutes the preconditions for a heterosexual development. Since the perception of the disharmony between instinctual impulses of the primary process and sexuality always results in causing insecurity within the sexual identity, an excessive cathexis of the sense of identity will provide the psychodynamic precondition for a solidly constructed heterosexuality. The cathexis has to be excessive, for only then can the polar contrast between male and female sexual roles have such an effect that it will replace the disharmony and so repress it that it disappears in the unconscious. It is important to me to show that in a heterosexual partnership, the disharmony between the instinctual impulses of the primary process and the sexual dictatorship is not solved or cancelled, but that it frequently is repressed by means of defense mechanisms, particularly by means of projection and delegation. In other words, also a heterosexual love relationship can flourish only if the enduring cathexis of the sexual object is freed from the tendency to a compulsive dependency on that object. If both partners, the woman as well as the man, succeed in this, the overcathexis of the polar contrast of the sexes is no longer necessary. Heterosexuality then loses its ideological character, and the sexual behavior, although it remains heterosexual, permits variations.

THE HOMOSEXUAL CAPABILITY TO LOVE

With manifest homosexuals, whether male or female, the circumstances are different. During autoerotic activity, the child grasps very early the possibility of maintaining a steadily repetitive, sexual cathexis and of doing away with the object dependence by making himself the sexual object. The autonomy the child thus experiences is subsequently overcathected and determines the development into homosexuality. With homosexuals, autoeroticism undergoes a change of function and serves dependency to maintain the autonomy vis-à-vis the sexual object, that is, it prevents the dependency on it. Since this experience of autonomy is the consequence of an overcathexis, it also is overestimated, and that evokes the danger of entering into sexual relationships with the conviction of preserving object independency. In reality, homosexuals, constantly tend to develop a compulsive object dependence on their sexual partners. When that occurs, the vicious circle develops much more quickly and perceptibly than it does with heterosexuals. The reason for this is, among others, that homosexuals can appeal to the available institutions of society only in a very limited way, because, on the one hand, the institutions are not meant for them and, on the other, they would scarcely know what to do with them. Obviously, the delegation of the dependency on the sexual object to the progeny is also not a consideration.

In order to oppose the vicious circle, the majority of homosexuals will not involve themselves with a dependency on the sexual object but, rather, will lead a promiscuous sexual life. In its attempt to understand homosexuals, psychoanalysis has made sexual behavior the center of its observation and has overlooked the nature of these people's problem.

The problem of homosexuals is that they can neither deepen the psychic relationships with their sexual partners nor can they differentiate these relationships—in proportion to their demands—without falling prey to the vicious circle of their sexual dictatorship. They cannot sufficiently maintain the sexual object cathexis because it threatens the dependency on the sexual object. In the analytic process, homosexuals tend to develop an object-related transference, and thereafter always tend to win the battle for object independency, because they are able to employ sexuality to prove their autonomy to the analytic partner by implying that the analytic partner is out of the question as a sexual object. Therefore it is important that the transference develop at the level of the instinctual impulses of the primary process, and that the analytic process not get stuck within the argumentations of the secondary process. When the analytic relationship is deepened by the emotional presence of both participants, a sexual dimension emerges very quickly and intensively in what takes place between analysand and analyst.

During the course of an analysis one homosexual remarked to me, "The only thing that really animates and interests me is the sexual. At every opportunity I think about the cock. I know this is the case with everybody, although most of them act as if it were otherwise. I would have stopped coming a long time ago if I hadn't known that you are exactly like me. Here this is so open and clear. I like that about you."

In order to understand the transference, one must recognize the unconscious motivations. Thus I told the analysand, "You like me because you feel that I like to be with you and talk with you, even though we won't do it together." The analysand: "But we could do it together. Maybe we should meet sometime in a sauna." After a short pause I said, "You expect me to be sexually excited when you come here, and to seduce you into sleeping with me. I don't believe you'd want that. You prefer doing it with your friends. After all, you've come to me for other reasons." The analysand: "At the beginning, certainly, but now it's different. With the men I do it with, I can't talk the way I talk to you. Homosexuals among themselves have very little to say to one another." I continued, "That's not true. Homosexuals can express themselves with great differentiation and enter into genuine love relationships. You can see that in our relationship, even though we don't sleep together." The analysand: "Once it gets that way with friends and we do it together, everything afterwards is quite different, noncommittal, and superficial. Then each one seeks another partner for the next night." "That is your experience," I said, "which explains why you fear that we might do it together." The analysand became visibly sad and moody and said: "Actually you are not at all interested in me. After all, you are married and have children and as an analyst you keep your distance from everything." This is the language of the secondary process, through which the sexual organization had been formed. It expresses the disappointment in the love object who constantly turns to other partners, other analysands, and with whom the deepening of the relationship cannot be permitted because of the threatening vicious circle.

Now it became essential to work this disappointing reaction through with the analysand and to show him that his disappointment had nothing at all to do with our relationship, but that, instead, it followed a repetition compulsion to reactivate, in the new relationship with me, experiences of disappointment reaching back into childhood. I interpreted to my analysand that he withdrew in disappointment because otherwise anxiety would appear, in connection with his attachment to me and his dependency on me. After that interpretation the analytical relationship became relaxed and the analysand was able to talk about his sexual fantasies, developed during masturbation, in which I became his homosexual partner. The analysand said: "When I reach orgasm, I feel good and am quite relaxed, because in my thoughts I have a long conversation with you and imagine we're making a long trip together." If the homosexual succeeds in speaking of his sexual fantasies in such a manner, and if he is emotionally in harmony with his partner, the analytic process develops further at the level of a primary-process exchange. However, if the analyst takes the attitude that he eventually would like to interpret to the analysand that his masturbatory fantasies are connected to his early childhood experiences and that, for instance, the analyst takes the place of the mother in the unconscious, he pursues considerations and interpretations of secondary-process events of which he frequently is not even conscious. The homosexual reacts to this with a withdrawal of his emotional movement and, by using his sexuality to do away with the partner on whom a dependency threatens to develop, gradually induces in the analytic relationship a struggle situation that is difficult to grasp.

I am not concerned here with demonstrating how an analytic process can be meaningfully developed. The clinical example was intended to illustrate that with the homosexual it is not a matter of changing the sexual organization, but rather of conserving it in such a way as to maintain the cathexis of the sexual object without falling victim to the vicious circle of the dependency on the sexual object. With homosexuals it becomes especially clear that the psychoanalytic relationship actually contains all the preconditions of a model relationship, in which the important thing is to maintain the libido cathexis, with its sexual implications, without bringing about a regression into a destructive dependency. The related, painful experiences analysands have to go through during their work of mourning make them conscious of the fact that the difficulties and conflicts they encounter in their homosexual lives are not based on their sexual organization but rather, as in all human beings, on a capability to love that is restricted or deprived of its potential. Thus, to help any person become capable of loving, it is not appropriate to manipulate his or her sexual life in one way or another, or to want to alter the person's sexual organization—including that of a homosexual.

PERVERSION AND THE ABILITY TO LOVE

What is striking in cases of perversion is an often extreme object dependency and a rigid object cathexis that is isolated from the emotional experience and has the effect of a foreign body in the personality. The perversions demonstrate in an extreme form the vicious circle between the repetition compulsion of the sexual cathexis and the dependency on the sexual object. Persons who develop a perversion have in early childhood fixated one of the polymorphous-perverse partial instincts to act as the support of a bridge that allows the instinctual impulses of the primary process permanent access to the experience. They have left an island for the dictatorship of sexuality where it can rage at will, while peace can be maintained within the rest of the domain. They do not repress the disharmony; instead, they experience it in the formation of their sexuality, which frequently does not fit their overall personality. They also do not fight object dependency; however, the communication with the instinctual impulses of the primary process is obtained at the cost of devitalizing their sexual objects. The perverse sexual organization ensures the emotional coherence of the personality by consuming all influences that might block it.

In the analytic process, perverts get involved with their partners only if a transference offer coming predominantly from the primary process is available. In their contact with other people, they shy away from object cathexes and object dependencies. If they permit them, they do so only seemingly, for in these cases specific material attributes of the person of reference are cathected, and dependencies are permitted by certain manipulations they expect or demand. With transsexuals this tendency is especially recognizable. The relationship with the physician or therapist is limited almost exclusively to the carrying out of the operative intervention to which one aspired.

If the relationship between the two partners in the analytic process is intensified on the basis of the unorganized, free-floating sexual aspects — that is, if it follows the instinctual impulses of the primary process — a process may develop in which the dictatorship of the sexuality is, as it were, fetched back off the island into its own domain. This step is already part of the development of the capability to love, which the pervert, like everyone else, has to accomplish if he wants to counter the destructive influences of the disharmony.

Samuel, a fetishist, whose sexuality was fixated on yellow boots and whose anxieties were related to the question of whether the boots would still suffice the next time he attempted to gratify himself sexually, had begun to feel comfortable during the analytic sessions, after months full of doubts and tensions. I sat behind him, and with what I said I merely indicated the direction in which we were moving. During one hour, in which I certainly had not interpreted anything, had neither uncovered any contexts nor encouraged or calmed Samuel's expectations with any sort of understanding words—during that hour, in which nothing solidly perceptible ever came to my mind, Samuel suddenly sat up, looked at me, and said, "If you understand so well what is going on inside me, then it has to be that sexually you are experiencing the same that I do." I answered Samuel, "The sexual is the same for you and me. Only the way sexuality develops over the course of one's lifetime corresponds to each person individually." Samuel agreed with me, and added, "It doesn't necessarily have to be yellow boots. I know somebody who does it with women's clothing." If Samuel believed he recognized in me a manifest fetishist, this was the expression of the secondary process coming to grips with the instinctual closeness the two of us had attained. The psychic climate, as Ferenczi once called it, in what took place between Samuel and me was determined by the instinctual impulses of the primary process. It was supported by the sexual, not by sexuality.

With perverts as with other people, the important thing is to interrupt the vicious circle between the repetition compulsion of the sexual cathexis and the subjugation to the sexual object, so that they can afford to maintain the sexual object cathexis without being dependent on the sexual object. Since Samuel's transference followed the instinctual impulses of the primary process, he started to cathect what we undertook together. He could address himself to whatever he thought fascinated me. What actually did fascinate me he did not know. He knew merely that it was not the boots. For him it was, and remained, the yellow boots, yet this did not interfere with our relationship. Our relationship followed precisely those tendencies of the primary process in which there are no conditions, no definite demands, no goals. In other words, with perverts it is not a matter of exchanging one object of their sexual fascination for another—for instance, the yellow boots for a homosexual or heterosexual partner—but rather of eradicating the extreme dependency on the yellow boots, although the fascination the yellow boots ignite in Samuel will be retained. Such a development is accompanied by a remobilization of severe conflicts and by much work of mourning, which reactivates the deprivation of love, the anxieties of object loss, and the separation problems of early childhood, until gradually the new viewpoint, developed from the emotional perception of the transference process, will prevail and make it possible to bring the capability to love into consciousness.

If the pervert attains this breakthrough, he by no means

relinquishes his perverse sexual organization: on the contrary, he keeps clinging to it. For the rest of his life, the yellow boot will remain the sexual object that emanates fascination; but at the same time, thanks to the influence of the instinctual impulses of the primary process, the pervert is in a position to find, through creative fantasy, the yellow boot in everything that animates him emotionally.

In the course of the analytic process, the primary-process emotional perception of the events of transference is—particularly so with perverts, but also with homosexuals and heterosexuals—the *via regia* for transforming the regressions resulting from the problems of dependency into regressions that serve the ego. Only when this is achieved will new, heretofore intractable instinctual impulses of the primary process be able to flow into the sexuality; by this means, new forms of dependency will emerge that in turn will bring about regressions which serve the ego and which will prevent further components of the id impulses from being stifled by the secondary process.

Under the dictatorship of sexuality—whatever shape it may take in the course of development: heterosexual, homosexual, autoerotic, perverse, passive-masochistic, aggressive, sadistic, promiscuous, religious-ascetic, animistic, mystic, or transcendental—the capability to love is subject to stress it can barely withstand. It can be developed and maintained only if the instinctual impulses of the primary process have a free, broad access to experience. In the psychosexual development of the human being, the primacy of the primary process has a disproportionately greater significance than the primacy of genitality, to which psychoanalysis assigns the central position.

8

THE FORMS OF INTERCOURSE OF PERVERSIONS AND THE PERVERSION OF THE FORMS OF INTERCOURSE: A LOOK OVER THE FENCE OF PSYCHOANALYSIS

Perversions are forms of intercourse. Fetishists, transvestites, sadists, masochists, paedophiles, pyromaniacs, exhibitionists, voyeurs, transsexuals, necrophiles, sodomists—I shall not describe them. I shall not seek to understand them psychoanalytically, nor do I want to compile old, familiar facts or add new ones to them. Perversions are sexual modes of experience that appear especially disconcerting and empathically forbidding, not merely because the sexual development of humans leads in the majority of instances to a heterosexual partner choice, but because, in the cultural and communal areas of certain societies, the psychic development from infant to adult suppresses the polymorphous-perverse character of human sexual life, and heterosexuality represents an ideological monopoly of such a society's morality.

Most things said about perversions are untruthful. What is called perversion is a myth. The only difference between anyone's experience that varies somewhat from the usual and the experience of a pervert is a difference of degree. In describing something as a perversion, one limits and distances oneself. Every society produces perversions and the perverts that it needs.

In Manhattan I discovered the colorfulness of New York in its blue-white-red chimneys behind the black and green facades of the skyscrapers. This colorfulness awakened a sensuous excitation in me. I was fascinated. During an analysis, a fetishist reported what takes place in him when he finally finds the long-sought yellow boots that excite and fascinate him. Can one compare these

130

two experiences? T. approaches me, reads what I have just written, and asks, "Was your impression of Manhattan really so strong that you can compare it with that of the fetishist—erection, orgasm, and all?" I say to T., "Do you know so exactly what happens in a fetishist when he is fascinated by the object of his longing? Do erection and orgasm take place at that point?"

The analogy is not pertinent. It contains a distortion. Regarded externally, a great difference exists between that fetishist and me in New York. He is seeking and finally finds what he seeks; I was surprised because I unexpectedly saw what I could not even begin to seek. Still, I say it is the same experience. It is a matter of having access to the grandiose. In all people, the luster of self-esteem bears the traces of the grandiose omnipotence of childhood. To succeed at that level of experience has little in common with the attainment of a goal.

When I exhibited my watercolors of American cities, one critic wrote, "He sees brilliant colors even in the gray stone deserts of New York or Chicago." Is that perverse? Certainly not. The perverse mode of experience represents a quantitative intensification and a sexual coloring of grandiosity. The pervert has a much more direct access to sensuality. However, this results in a qualitatively altered intercourse with sensuality, which is no longer adapted to reality. In general, children have a much more direct access to perversity than adults. Any single trait in their sexual games is less characteristic than the direct, open access to sensuality.

A child analyst, approximately forty years old, telephoned me in great excitement. She demanded a meeting with me about a peculiar case in her analytic practice. She made a five-hour train trip and appeared at the appointed time. She wept, she was perplexed. For more than two years she had been analyzing an eight-year-old boy, a "social misfit." Meanwhile, the boy had become unobtrusive. He was an intelligent, wide-awake boy full of imagination, far advanced for his age. Recently he had come to a session and demanded that his analyst explain to him exactly what happens when the bull mounts the cow from behind. The analyst tried to offer the boy sexual enlightenment. At the end of the hour he said, "If you don't want to tell me what happens when the bull mounts the cow, I'll ask the people in the street." At the following session, the same thing happened. The analyst became ever more helpless, the boy ever more defiant, almost physically aggressive. At that stage the woman rushed to see me. I: "Why are you weeping?" The analyst: "I should never have become a child analyst. I don't understand children." I: "You are an excellent analyst. You just didn't understand that with his question about bull and cow the boy wanted to know whether you, his analyst, had already had sexual intercourse, whether you have a man to whom you make love. He does know you're not married and that you have no children."

When our meeting ended, the woman felt anxious about the next session with the boy. "What shall I tell him? Should I tell him the truth? Is that still analytic?" The next session took a completely unexpected turn. The boy was relaxed and did not ask again. It was as if he had been present during our discussion.

The serious in playfulness and the playful in seriousness are traits of the mode of experience that give the grandiose being access to self-esteem without the appearance of shame, maladaptation, or agonizing self-destruction. When the boy addressed the analyst's intimate sexual realm, the playful aspect in her got lost. Everything was now deadly serious. A deep trench opened up—as is quite common in our performance-oriented society—between the playful and the serious. Since people are brought up to experience the "seriousness of life" in the work process, it is not really surprising that the playful aspect in recreation merely amounts to a frantic, compensatory balancing act. Daily life becomes gray, sensuality is missing. The relationship between society and perverts can be compared with the analyst and the cow-and-bull boy. The inability to approach and comprehend the playful aspect seriously, and the serious aspect playfully, results in a mendacity that covers up a deeply rooted helplessness. Society feels threatened by manifest perversions because they address those of its microstructures which are perverse the same way the boy addressed the sexual realm of his analyst. In society, this results in misunderstandings, hostility, and devaluation in the judgment of perversion.

Psychoanalysis has always attempted to comprehend perversions in their essence and to make the fate the instincts underwent in childhood responsible for the development of any type of sexual behavior in the adult. Psychoanalysis has contributed a great deal to the clarification of these questions. But it has failed in the aim to which it aspired, namely, to heal the psychically ill of their sexual aberrations, of those deviations from the norm which caused illness. At the same time, this only covers up another problem: psychoanalysis actually has no goal. Only psychoanalysts aspire to goals because they think in conformity with society. To the extent that it serves the interests of a ruling society, psychoanalysis has forfeited much of its actual substance. It has even adopted the forms of intercourse of a society in which it was developed and must prove itself. It perfects and sharpens its scientific instrument with the same seriousness as the society in which it operates increases and differentiates the means of production, without taking into consideration the psychic effect on the consumer in all its consequences. The absurdity permeating this whole endeavor is denied, yet it is identical with the perverse that in secret permeates "normal" people's forms of intercourse. True, psychoanalysis discovered the polymorphous-perverse aspects of infantile sexuality and, thanks to this knowledge, also manages to reveal through its work the fate the instincts undergo in those to whom it addresses itself; however, the more it has adapted to the roles assigned to it by society, the more it has become unable to recognize the absurd within itself. The playful, in its serious effort, seems suspicious to psychoanalysis. The seriousness in the play receives less and less attention because it no longer corresponds to society's standards of evaluation. And yet, psychoanalysis is supposed to be the science of the unconscious. The seriousness with which it pursues the scientific determination of its subject ought to be permeated by playful pleasure in order that the potential possibilities of people may be perceived in their entirety, and to everything that had seemed fixed up to now may be related anew, expanded, reformulated, and comprehended differently. The results of such a process would correspond with the seriousness that forms the base of all true play. In the intercourse forms of psychoanalysis, a chasm between play and seriousness is becoming increasingly apparent, just as it is in the society we live in. Psychoanalysis applies the same measures to its activities, scientifically and practically, that our performance-oriented society applies to the work ethic. Since the behavior patterns of psychoanalysis also convey the myth of omniscience, its representatives enjoy high social prestige. The elitist consciousness that goes with this prestige represents the grandiose self in the same rigid, almost ritualized manner in which, because of its disconcerting sexual admixture, it is concealed in the perverse ritual.

I compared the colorfulness of Manhattan with the yellow boot of the shoe-fetishist in order to detach the perverse from our fixated notions of fetishism. The fixated object, "the yellow boot," is emotional stimulus become rigid, and this rigidity has a deep significance in the experience of the person who has become a fetishist. The gap between the serious and the playful is evident here, too. The ritualization of a perverse activity reflects the loss of the playful in a phenomenon that must be taken seriously. Yet, the same society that judges the pervert treats the human being like a plaything it cannot take seriously.

Everybody has a self-image, and this image must by nice and well-rounded, to provide the self-esteem with strength and capability of resistance in order to be able to bear the realities of life and the society in which they live. Now, this image we have built up of ourselves is the result of a long development, which began early in our lives and was guided early into decisive, highly specific channels. With the fetishist of whom I spoke, the yellow boot is a part of the image of himself. When life begins, mother and infant are a unit, each a part of the other. But it cannot remain that way. Inevitably, a disturbance of this dual-unionistic self-containment occurs. The world of the infant is then no longer perfect. Something is missing. A gap, a rip, a chasm appears, which creates anxieties that result in an inordinate desire to alleviate this disturbance, this thing that is missing. Fantasies of omnipotence and delusions of grandeur attempt to repair the completeness of the infant's world by excluding the reality of experience. That cannot succeed. Under the pressure of reality, the fantasies of omnipotence and grandeur are transformed into movement, into energy that is to serve the fulfillment of ideals. In the dualistic union, the infant was simply satisfied—in love, so to speak, with satisfaction. Later on it falls in love with the person providing satisfaction and idealizes the great figures of its environment. It also becomes more conscious of reality and internalizes the admiration, which, for the time being, is directed outside. Now it starts discovering things about itself that it admires. Thus the image of one's own inner person emerges, which must be rounded out, self-contained, and beautiful. However, this rounded-out, self-contained, beautiful image of one's self almost never materializes. All human beings experience a failure during this process. In what they think, fantasize, do, and creatively form, they strive to fill the gap, round out the self-containment, and produce the beauty of the their self-image. If such striving becomes conscious aim, either a sense of deepest shame or an undifferentiated arrogance arises. Both are unbearable in the long run. In all events, the tendency remains unconscious, aimless. There are many ways leading to what will never be more than an approximation.

The gap in the self-esteem creates an agonizing, self-destructive tension that robs the expression of the self-esteem of all sensuality. Psychoanalysis sees in this a structural disturbance of the narcissistic development in early childhood, which has far-reaching ill effects in the formation of the personality. Psychoanalysis early on recognized the significance of infantile sexuality as the expression of sexuality's polymorphous-perverse, naturally preconditioned structure. The polymorphous-perverse aspect is in all instances somehow built into the self-image of the person, and the role it plays in the development into heterosexuality—a development so highly cathected in our society—is as great as the role it plays in all other forms of sexual experience that are frowned upon.

During childhood, the traits of the sexual predisposition still inform, without contradiction, all activities, all fantasizing and creating. Because of that, parts of infantile sexuality always have a share in the image of one's own self during the various developmental stages of childhood. Since infantile sexuality usually has a polymorphous-perverse structure, one may also say that children have a direct, naive access to the perverse. This access becomes less visible once they are adults. This is similarly true in regard to certain talents. There are children who paint and draw as if a secret Klee or Picasso were concealed within them. With the onset of puberty, the talent fades and makes room for other movements. One need not regret this.

There are people who during their childhood discover somehow and sometime, always quite early and inexplicably, a sharply delineated trait of perverse fascination. At a decisive stage, they build this discovered, overevaluated aspect accurately, like some colorful stone, into the mosaic of the image of themselves. In the course of their further development, usually with the onset of puberty, this sharply delineated trait of perverse fascination might fade and make room for other movements. However, the discovery of such a sharply delineated trait of perverse fascination cannot be compared with a talent, but rather with what a talent uniquely creates. A talent is a delightful game that aims at expressing experience creatively, but it never represents the only way to express experience in general.

When roles must be assumed, when institutions and formalizations begin to codetermine the experience, when, that is, heads are forced into line by society, talents may fade, because people's fantasies are usually not forced into line that easily. The possibilities exist, however, that under new and different circumstances such talents may be revived.

A sharply delineated trait of perverse fascination is the outcome of a creative accomplishment that at one time, very early, was brought about through a threatening situation. Individual traits of the polymorphous-perverse sexual predisposition were emphasized, further developed, differentiated, and, like a stopper, installed as seamlessly as possible into the threatening gap in the self-esteem. A void was thus filled in the image of one's own self, in order to avoid a rupture in the image of one's own person. Such a rupture would have resulted in a mode of experience that would have oscillated between a disjointed omnipotence and a helpless, inner emptiness. This stopper formation in a person's realm of experience has the disturbing effect of a foreign body, comparable to a prosthesis. And yet, the comparison with a prosthesis is misleading. The perverse trait is a living part of the person, since it contains, quite simply, the sexual instinctuality. The comparison with a prosthesis, however, is appropriate if one considers the societal forms of intercourse in which perversions are exercised. If roles have to be assumed, if institutions and formalizations begin to codetermine the experience, then the perverse, isolated trait in the experience of the affected people becomes more sharply defined and turns into a perversion. The ritualization of the perverse action increases the sensation of a foreign body. The rigidity maintains the balance with the adaptation demanded by society, or even partially replaces it. The assumption of roles, the institutionalizations, formalizations, and the societally conditioned manipulations contain the perverse microstructure of "normal" persons' forms of intercourse. A reinforced echo-effect develops on both sides: the pervert reinforces his perversion; society intensifies its attitude and ritualizes its forms of intercourse vis-à-vis the pervert.

This need not necessarily be so. In foreign cultures there are social structures that develop quite different forms of intercourse, in which the previously described polarization does not find expression to the same degree. I have found cultures in Papua, New Guinea, but also in Madagascar, where the very access to animistic modes of experience makes it possible for the polymorphous-perverse background of the human psyche to be included in all activities, all creating and thinking, and to be expressed in the most varied forms. In these cultures, rituals can be joyous festivities that permit the participation in sensual pleasures in a playful manner, whereas the rituals of our own society are usually cold and without any inner, sensual participation on the part of the individual.

In Madagascar there are peoples who bury many of their dead in a special way. One ethnic group in the southwest of the island cultivates this custom: Near the river, the daughters of a socially important man who has died cut the flesh off the bones of the corpse and clean the skeleton until it is snow-white. The bones are then separated from one another and placed into a small coffin, which is buried with special ceremonies. A neighboring ethnic group buries its dead in huge piles of stone, which are decorated with wooden steles and statuettes that represent scenes from the life of the deceased. On the high plateau in the center of the island, particularly colorful houses are constructed, usually situated at the top of the hill, that contain the coffin with the corpse. Once a year, the coffin is brought out and carried about for the entire day. Several men bear it on their shoulders, purposely tripping so that family members and everyone accompanying the procession can hear the rattling of the bones. A joyous, festive mood prevails. In our society, such treatment of the dead would be condemned as a desecration of the dead committed by perverse necrophiles.

In the middle Sepik district of New Guinea, numerous deep cuts are inflicted into the backs of the young men during their initiation, so that the bad blood can flow out. With women such a procedure is superfluous, since they menstruate. On the occasion of the initiation festivities, which take place after the healing of the wounds, certain members of the initiate's family appear in prescribed roles corresponding to old customs. The men appear in women's clothing and the women in men's clothing. This institutionalized transvestism is an integrating component of the cultural and social consciousness of that population. In our society, such occurrences would be designated as the sadistic actions of transvestite psychopaths.

In both examples it is striking to see how well the people of these cultures understand to take a relaxed, playful attitude towards perverse forms of acting, thinking, and experiencing. The contrast with similarly perverse forms of intercourse in our culture arises perhaps less from the thematically demonstrable perverse traits of any given behavior — which can be found in every human society, even though not everywhere so openly apparent — than from the way these forms of intercourse are handled. In those societies, everything seems playful, easy, and relaxed when people are confronted with their own perverse modes of experience and with those of others. In our society, perverse modes of experience result in tense and frozen forms of intercourse for the experiencers themselves and for everyone else confronted by such experiences. The related loss of the playful aspect has the effect that the pleasure in the animation of infantile fantasies, which greatly inflate the self-esteem, becomes degraded so that it appears absurd and ludicrous.

In all perversions, the discovery in early childhood of a sharply delineated trait of perverse fascination was also the discovery of a splendid possibility to powerfully animate the miserable self-esteem that was threatened by an inner emptiness. For that reason one may also say that a perverse fascination opens up an avenue to the grandiose. In childhood such fantasies of omnipotence are still free of contradictions and linked to a sensual attaining of pleasure.

In the foreign cultures mentioned, forms of intercourse have developed that maintain and integrate this gaining of pleasure by means of the perverse. Because of that, the polar contrasts between perverse and normal forms of intercourse are hardly apparent. In our society, the corresponding forms of intercourse are rigid and without pleasure. Their ritualizations are often emotionally drained. This results in the devaluation of everything perverse as ridiculous and absurd. We can thus understand the influence of societal structures upon the formation of perversions. In this view the emphasis is not on any particular sexual practice but rather on the sensual expression that any given experience does, or does not, produce.

Sensuality is not identical with sexuality. Neither can one say that a certain mode of activity or a certain choice of occupation is more sensual than another. Everything can acquire a sensual radiation if what we do, or the way we do it, rounds out and beautifies our own image in our self-esteem to such an extent that a relaxed basic mood emerges within us, a mood that is the very precondition for allowing us, through an oscillating, playful erotism, to seduce others into approaching us.

Thanks to their socially adequate role behavior, it may well be easier for bank employees, car salesmen, bicyclists, psychoanalysts, greengrocers, film distributors, heterosexuals, husbands, anti-authoritarian educators, and policemen to develop a well-balanced sense of self-esteem in their activities. Whether or not there emerges in these people the relaxed basic mood that engenders true sensuality depends on the level of mendacity admixed with their self-evaluation. It is much more difficult for perverts, homosexuals, male prostitutes, whores, junkies, and youths who refuse to accept a role society offers, to create a well-rounded, beautiful image of themselves and to hold on to it. If they can, however, then they have managed it in a much more autonomous way than their fellow human beings who are adapted to society. Success in this sense is very rare. In these people mendacity is much easier to see and more brutally punished. Their desperation appears as sickness.

The psychoanalysis of perverts and other "social misfits" can decisively further, or effect, a development to a tenable, rounded-out self-esteem, which includes the sexual mode of experience, be that of a perverse or another nature. Only, the psychoanalyst must not fight the perversion, the "social error," as something disturbing or sick. What appears as sickness was once the "colorful stone" that was found and added into the mosaic of one's inner image so that this image shone and continued to exist. There was no choice, and if the price had to be paid in the form of a freezing of sensual experience, there was always the possibility of getting what was frozen to move again sometime later. Renunciation of the "colorful stone" would have meant decay, psychic incoherence, or a genuine, possibly incurable illness.

In the practice of psychoanalysis, one experiences that in this way: the relaxed basic mood, which eventually flows into the anxiously guarded perverse structure of psychical experience, emerges, to begin with and under all circumstances, in the slowly deepening relationship between the psychoanalyst and the analysand. In order to make that possible at all, analysts must be conscious of their own profound conflictual tendencies and must not deny them. Only through their own personal analyses were they able to experience that consciousness. However, this experience showed them that their own conflictuality, permeated in its own way by perverse tendencies, cannot be eradicated by any means. The experience of one's own personal analysis is the experience of being limited, of being restricted to what little one can change. Most things by far are simply the way they are. Only flexibility in dealing with them and elasticity in the valuation of one's own inner and outer demands, which everyone makes upon oneself, will create new formulations that put things into relation to one another, expand modes of observation, and permit a different comprehension of things that up to then had been rigidly fixed.

One of my very first analysands was a feeble-minded male. I worked at a clinic at that time. Paul L. was so retarded that he could comprehend only the simplest linear connection of cause and effect, such as: My father was very strict, therefore I had to work all the time. Or: The soup was too hot; I couldn't eat it. Paul L. was in analysis with me for three and a half years, three hours a week. After three years he came to a session, sat at my table, laid his head on his arm and wept for a long time. Then he said, "Now

I've found out: I'm feeble-minded." He wept almost the entire hour. I sat next to him, speechless. Paul L. went home after the hour and said to his wife, "You and I, we're both feeble-minded. We will not have children, otherwise something bad will happen." In the course of the following months, Paul L. became foreman in a gardener's nursery. He worked there the entire winter because he was so industrious and considerate. He had four workers under him, whom he supervised. He could neither read nor write. One of his workers did that for him.

Owing to Paul L. and our mutual experience, I saw over the fence of psychoanalysis for the first time. How is one to understand that? Must one analyze a feeble-minded person in order to understand psychoanalysis? Or is the comparison intended to mean that perverts should be treated like the feeble-minded? One can misunderstand everything, all the time.

Feeble-minded Paul L. perceived the most improbable thing—that what was taken for granted for others was unattainable for him. It also was the most immutable thing, that which simply is. In the playful relationship he perceived the serious. He then proceeded to deal with playful wisdom with the serious fact of his retardation. He became another person, all the time himself, feeble-minded, to be sure, but different. The feeble-mindedness of Paul L. in my example is merely an extreme expression of what, after all, goes on in every analysis. It certainly need not be a case of feeble-mindedness, where self-recognition is difficult to imagine anyway because of the mental deficiency. In any case it is a long process until the seriousness of self-recognition of one's own limitations is joined by the playful. For the activities of the psycho-analyst this self-recognition is a prerequisite. For the analysand, most especially for the pervert in analysis, it will be crucial to press forward towards such self-recognition.

The psychoanalyst establishes a relationship with the analysand that primarily suits the analyst, not the analysand. Only that way can the relationship be really correct. It is correct in regard to what goes on within the analyst. If such a relationship exists, the analysand will develop an ever more comprehensive emotional echo, supported by deep feelings, which sets into motion everything in him or her that had once become rigid. In the course of this process, however, the unfathomable liveliness of the partner, in our case a pervert, becomes the great manipulator of the other, the analyst. Therefore it is not enough for analysts to look within themselves and maintain and intensify a harmonious relationship with their analysands. They cannot withdraw from the enormous seduction emanating from their partners, but they can certainly become conscious of it. The point is to transform the gruesome into the serious, and manipulations into play. Healthy human understanding is not enough. Experience and a bag of methodological tricks are not reliable sources of support, since the pervert's forms of intercourse reactivate the secret and hidden perverse traits of the normal person's forms of intercourse.

Psychoanalysis as a science has created a finely structured, profound theory: metapsychology. In addition it has described concepts of a theory of psychoanalytic technique. Metapsychology and psychoanalytic theory of technique are not systems of rules, applicable in certain situations for certain purposes to attain certain aims. They can in fact be abused in that connection, if one thinks positivistically. Positivistic thinking is the basis of economic success in our society, the ideology of the performance-conscious human, the instrument of those who rule, the essence of power. Positivistic psychoanalysis wants to differentiate between the healthy and the sick, help those who suffer realize their objectives, cure everything that appears sick. However, practicing psychoanalysis means thinking dialectically, and dialectically understanding and applying the scientific theories psychoanalysis has created. These theories serve analysts in maintaining their relaxed basic mood. This is possible only if the relaxation of the analysand during interpretive work has an effect on the analyst in turn. In such interaction, the unconscious becomes conscious when the quantitative accumulation of certain ideational contents, conditioned by the situation, undergoes a qualitative transformation that unexpectedly raises things that seem to have been understood to a new level of comprehension.

I shall not attempt to clarify the process that makes perverts remain perverse without being perverse the way all of us are, without exactly knowing it. Rather, let me paraphrase—metaphorically, as it were—the perverse form of intercourse of the "normal" person and, in so doing, look over the fence of psychoanalysis, over the fence of the prevailing forms of intercourse, and over the fence that separates perverse people from others. The analogy I use is applicable to anyone, regardless of his or her professional or social position or his or her form of sexuality. I am not concerned with setting up a program, or an objective, but rather in trying to give a graphic portrayal of a dialectical interaction.

In a psychiatric clinic, a physician observes a mentally ill woman for several months. For over ten years she has lived in the institution, and for years she has been unable to do anything but go to a window every morning and stare into the courtyard. She sees nothing in that courtyard. She no longer experiences anything, she is unapproachable, motionless, rigid, and mute. The physician begins to devote even more time to this woman. He hovers around her, appears late at night and early in the morning, when the patients are still in their dormitories, and tries to start a dialog with her. Everything seems hopeless. One evening the physician suddenly turns to the woman, who is standing at the window as usual, and tells her with great urgency that he had observed her without interruption all night and all day. The physician himself cannot explain how he came to react in this manner. The woman is completely astonished, turns around, and starts speaking with the physician. She is completely changed and the next morning begins working in the laundry.

I have no intention of finding a psychiatric, let alone a psychoanalytic explanation of this episode. I wish to compare this vignette with the relationship society establishes with the pervert. Fundamentally, society and all its members who see themselves as normal regard perverts with the same rigid look with which that woman stared into the courtyard. They all discern nothing in the perverse; they experience nothing in their contacts with it, they are emotionally unapproachable, rigid, and mute. In my comparison, the physician—absurd as this may sound—is the pervert. The pervert exists in a society that cultivates forms of experience and intercourse foreign to him but to which he has accustomed himself. I believe that in this regard he is comparable to the physician in the psychiatric institution, because that physician, too, feels the forms of experience and of intercourse as disconcerting, even though he has accustomed himself to them through his professional activities. The private life of the physician follows different forms of experience and of intercourse, namely those which correspond to himself. Analogously, the "private life" of the pervert contrasts with the forms of intercourse of "normal" people. The pervert's forms of intercourse are rituals of his sexual practices that correspond to him. The institutional life of patients is shut off and usually has little or, if possible, nothing in common with the private life of the physician.

In my example something special happens. The physician begins to get interested in the mentally ill woman in a manner that actually corresponds much more to the forms of experience and intercourse of his own private life than to those practiced by the patients in the institution. That is unusual. A playful tendency begins to animate the professional ritual of his psychiatric activity in a special way. He hovers around the woman, long given up as incurable, with an almost childlike curiosity and develops a fantasy that greatly inflates his self-esteem. He wants to attempt the most improbable thing of all: reestablish a dialog with this unapproachable patient. He seeks admission to the omnipotence and finds it by calling out to the sick woman that he had stared at her without interruption in exactly the same way she constantly stared into the courtyard. He has thus made the forms of experience and intercourse of the mentally ill in the institution into his own forms without giving up or even changing his own, very different forms. He has remained exactly the same he always was. Also, he did not assume a new role. He has acted without artifice or mendacity. He did not suddenly take the sick woman unawares or trick her; instead, he succeeded in establishing a dialog. He loosened up the playful aspect of his omnipotence fantasy and the serious aspect of his partner's illness by playful means. This way he found the avenue to dialog, whereupon the sick woman abandoned her rigidity and made the physician's forms of experience and intercourse corresponding to the physician's private life into her own forms. In the process she remains the same person she always was. She too has taken on no new role, has not reacted with artifice or mendacity. She feels neither caught unawares nor tricked, but instead resumes the dialog she conducted previously with other people. She has only given up the disconcerting, rigid, ritualized forms of experience and intercourse that had brought her and all the other patients into the institution.

If I now follow my analogy through to the end, the pervert would be the person seeking the dialog with the other, the normal person. He hovers around normal people and tries over and over again to approach them. If he were able, following the example of the physician in our account, to press playfully forward into normal society with his private, that is, perverse forms of experience and intercourse, something unusual would emerge. He might succeed, as the physician did, in suddenly approaching the deeply buried, frozen, perverse in the normal person. He would sense a feeling of empathy in his new partner, or a radiance in the partner's expression, which in turn would stir something in him. He would be enriched, just as the physician felt enriched by his experience with the woman.

With this challenging analogy I want to suggest that if so-called normal persons, with their polymorphous-perverse structures, can only look at a pervert the way the sick woman stared at the courtyard of the clinic, then, as a rule, something must be stirred up inside them to make them aware. Something must happen to them that they least expected, namely, that they suddenly become involved in an affective dialog with a person who has a playful, relaxed way with the perverse and yet is in no way especially obtrusive, and that they thus unexpectedly enter into forms of experience and intercourse that are simply not provided for in "normal" people, even though nothing striking separates those forms from the normal forms. It is precisely because they permit themselves to get involved and step beyond the fence of the so-called forms of intercourse that they find playful access to their own perverse traits and can recognize these traits in the other person. Something may then occur within these people that may be disquieting, since it might not appear normal to them. But precisely that is necessary in order to transform and expand the "normal" contained in the perverse into something beyond that "normal" that is healthy.

In conclusion, and to be just, I must ask what will happen to perverts who can look at their own perversion only in the way the sick woman looked at the courtyard of the clinic. The same thing will happen to them that happened to the so-called normal person and that they least expected, namely, that they are unexpectedly included in an affective dialog and that they take part in forms of intercourse simply not provided for in perverts. They feel disquieted because these forms deviate strikingly from those they pursued previously. But precisely because they permit themselves to get involved and step beyond the fence of perversion, they find playful access to traits of their own personality that are not perverse at all, and they can compare these with similar traits in others. It may then happen that something occurs within these people that is disquieting because it no longer appears perverse to them.

References

Bak, R. C. (1953): Fetishism, in: *J. Amer. Psa. Assn.* 1 (S. 285-298)

Balint, E. (1963): On being empty of oneself, in: *Int. J. Psa.* 44 (470-480)

Barande, I (1968): Le vu et l'entendu dans la cure, in: *Revue Franç. de Psa.* 32 (67-84)

Chasseguet-Smirgel, J. (1964): *Recherches psychanalytiques nouvelles sur la sexualité féminine,* Payot, Paris

Dannecker M. und R. Reiche (1974): *Der gewöhnliche Homosexuelle,* S. Fischer, Frankfurt/M.

Devereux, G. (1967): La renonciation à l'identité: défense contre l'anéantissement, in: *Revue Franç. de Psa.* 31 (101-142)

Erdheim, M. (1982): *Die gesellschaftliche Produktion von Unbewußtheit,* Suhrkamp, Frankfurt/M.

Erikson, E. H. (1956): The problem of identity, in: *J. Amer. Psa. Assn.* 4 (56-121)

Ferenczi, S. (1939): *Bausteine zur Psychoanalyse,* Huber, Bern

Freud, A. (1968): *Wege und Irrwege in der Kinderentwicklung,* Huber/Klett, Bern und Stuttgart

Freud, S. (1900): The interpretation of dreams, in: *Standard Edition* 4 & 5

—— (1905): Three essays on the theory of sexuality, in: *Standard Edition* 7 (135-243)

—— (1914): On narcissism: an introduction, in: *Standard Edition* 14 (117-140)

—— (1920a): Beyond the pleasure principle, in: *Standard Edition,* 18 (7-64)

—— (1920b): The psychogenesis of a case of homosexuality in a woman, in: *Standard Edition* 18 (145-172)

—— (1933): New introductory lectures on psycho-analysis, in: *Standard Edition* 22 (5-182)

—— (1940): Splitting of the ego in the process of defence, in: *Standard Edition* 23 (271-278).

145

Gillespie, W. H. (1952): Notes on the analysis of sexual perversions, in: *Int. J. Psa.* 33 (S. 397–402)

—— (1964): Symposium on Homosexuality, in: *Int. J. Psa.* 45 (203–209)

Giovacchini, P. L. (1963): Integrative aspects of object relationship, in: *Psychoanal. Quart.* 32 (393–407)

Glover, E. (1933): The relation of perversion formation to the development of reality sense, in: *Int. J. Psa.* 14 (486–504)

Greenacre, P. (1953): Certain relationships between fetishism and the faulty development of the body image, in: *Psychoanalytic Study of the Child* 8 (S. 79–98)

—— (1955): Further considerations regarding fetishism, in: *Psychoanalytic Study of the Child* 10 (187–194)

—— (1958): Early physical determinants in the development of sense of identity, in: *J. Amer. Psa. Assn.* 6 (612–627)

—— (1960): Further notes on fetishism, in: *Psychoanalytic Study of the Child* 15 (191–207)

Greenson, R. R. (1965): Homosexualité et identité sexuelle, in: *Revue Franç. de Psa.* 29 (343–348)

Grinberg, L., M. Langer, D. Libermann, E. und G. T. de Rodrigué (1967): The psychoanalytic process, in: *Int. J. de Psa.* 48 (498–503)

Grunberger, B. (1964): De l'image phallique, in: *Revue Franç. de Psa.* 28 (217–234)

Hartmann, H. (1954): Problems of infantile neurosis. A discussion (Arden House Symposium), in: *Psychoanalytic Study of the Child* 9 (31–36)

Jacobson, E. (1964): *The Self and the Object World,* International Universities Press, New York

Kernberg, O. F. (1977): Normaler und pathologischer Narzißmus im Wandel", in: *Psychoanalyse im Wandel,* Suhrkamp, Frankfurt/M.

Kestenberg, J. S. (1956): On the development of maternal feelings in early childhood, in: *Psychoanalytic Study of the Child* 11 (257–291)

—— (1956): Vicissitudes of female sexuality, in: *J. Amer. Psa. Assn.* 4 (453–476)

—— (1965/1967): The role of movement patterns in development: I. Rhythms of movement; II. Flow of tension and effort; III. The control of shape, in: *Psychoanal. Quart.* 34 (1–36); 34 (517–563); 36 (356–409)

—— (1967/1968): Phases of adolescence: with suggestions for a correlation of psychic and hormonal organization. Parts I, II, III, in: *J. Amer. Acad. Child Psychiat.* 6 (426–463); 6 (577–614); 7 (108–151)

—— (1968): Outside and inside, male and female, in: *J. Amer. Psa. Assn.* 16 (457–520)

Kohut, H. (1966): Formen und Umformungen des Narzißmus", in: *Psyche* 20 (561–587)

—— (1969): Die psychoanalytische Behandlung narzißtischer Persönlichkeitsstörungen", in: *Psyche* 23 (321)

—— (1971a): *Narzißmus,* Suhrkamp, Frankfurt/M. 1973

—— (1971b): *The analysis of the self,* International Universities Press, New York

—— (1977): *The restoration of the self,* International Universities Press, New York. Deutsch: *Die Heilung des Selbst,* Suhrkamp, Frankfurt/M. 1979

Kris, E. (1952): Comments on Spontaneous Artistic Creations by Psychotics, in: *Psychoanalytic Explorations in Art,* New York

Langer, M. (1964): Symptom formation and character formation, in: *Int. J. Psa.* 45 (158–160)

Lampl-de Groot, J. (1967): On obstacles standing in the way of psychoanalytic cure, in: *Psychoanalytic Study of the Child* 22 (20–35)

Lincke, H. (1981): *Instinktverlust und Symbolbildung,* Hrsg. Hans-Jürgen Heinrichs, Severin & Siedler, Berlin

Lipin, T. (1963): The repetition compulsion and "maturational" drive-representatives, in: *Int. J. Psa.* 44 (389–406)

Lomas, P. (1965): Passivity and failure of identity development, in: *Int. J. Psa.* 46 (438–454)

Lorand, S. und M. Balint (1956): *Perversions, Psychodynamics and Therapy,* Random House, New York

Mahler, M. S. (1958): Autism and symbiosis. Two extreme disturbances of identity, in: *Int. J. Psa.* (77–83)

—— (1969): *On human symbiosis and the vicissitudes of individuation,* Hogarth Press, London

Moore, B. E. (1961): Frigidity in women (Report), in: *J. Amer. Psa. Assn.* 9 (571–584)

Pasche, F. (1964): Symposium on homosexuality, in: *Int. J. Psa.* 45 (210–213)

Rapaport, D. (1958): The theory of ego autonomy: a generalization, in: *Bull. Menninger Clin.* 22 (13–35)

—— (1960): The structure of psychoanalytic theory: a systemizing attempt, in: *Psychological Issues, Monogr. 6,* International Universities Press, New York

—— (1967): *The Collected Papers of David Rapaport,* New York

Reich, A. (1960): Pathologic forms of self-esteem regulation, in: *Psychoanalytic Study of the Child* 15 (S. 215–232)

Rose, G. J. (1966): Body and ego reality, in: *Int. J. Psa.* 47 (502–509)

Rosenfeld, H. (1949): Remarks on the relation of male homosexuality to paranoia, paranoic anxiety, and narcissism, in: *Int. J. Psa.* 30 (36–47)

Rubinfine, D. L. (1958): Panel report: Problems of identity, in: *J. Amer. Psa. Assn.* 6 (131–142)

Sandler, J. und B. Rosenblatt (1962): The concept of the representational world, in: *Psychoanalytic Study of the Child* 17 (128–145)

Sarlin, C. N. (1963): Feminine identity, in: *J. Amer. Psa. Assn.* 11 (790–816)

Saul, L. J. und S. L. Warner (1967): Identity and a point of technique, in: *Psychoanal. Quart.* 36 (532–545)

Socarides, C. W. (1968): *The Overt Homosexual,* Grune & Stratton, New York and London. Deutsch: *Der offene Homosexuelle,* Suhrkamp, Frankfurt/M. 1971

Spitz, R. A. (1962): Autoerotism re-examined: The role of early sexual behaviour patterns in personality formation, in: *Psychoanalytic Study of the Child* 17 (283–315). Deutsch: Ein Nachtrag zum Problem des Autoerotismus", in: *Psyche* 18 (241–272)

—— (1965): *The First Year of Life. A Psychoanalytic Study of Normal and Deviant Development of Object Relations,* New York

Stoller, R. J. (1964/1968): A contribution to the study of gender identity/A further contribution to the study of gender identity, in: *Int. J. Psa.* 45 (220–225); 49 (364–368)

Vinnai, G. (1977): *Das Elend der Männlichkeit,* Rowohlt, Reinbek

Weissmann, Ph. (1962): Structural considerations in overt male bisexuality, in: *Int. J. Psa.* 34 (89–97)

Wiedemann, G. H. (1962): Survey of psychoanalytic literature on overt male homosexuality", in: *J. Amer. Psa. Assn.* 10 (386–409)

Winnicott, D. W. (1953): Transitional objects and transitional phenomena, in: *Int. J. Psa.* 34 (89–97). Deutsch: Übergangsobjekte und Übergangsphänomene, in: *Psyche* 23 (666–682)